Finding Nevo

Nevo Zisin

Finding Nevo

How I Confused Everyone

WALKER BOOKS
AND SUBSIDIARIES
LONDON • BOSTON • SYDNEY • AUCKLAND

First published in 2017 by Walker Books Australia Pty Ltd
Locked Bag 22, Newtown, NSW 2042 Australia
www.walkerbooks.com.au

This edition published in 2020.

A catalogue record for this book is available from the National Library of Australia

ISBN: 978 1 925381 18 4

Typeset in Garamond
Printed and bound in Australia by Griffin Press

15 14 13 12

The paper this book is printed on is certified against the Forest Stewardship Council® Standards. Griffin Press holds FSC chain of custody certification SGS-COC-005088. FSC promotes environmentally responsible, socially beneficial and economically viable management of the world's forests.

This book was written on and based in Naarm. I want to acknowledge the true custodians, the Boon Wurrung and Wurundjeri people of the Kulin Nation. I'd like to pay my respect to Elders past and present, and any Indigenous individuals reading this book. Sovereignty has never been ceded.

I would like to dedicate this book to the LGBTQIA+ elders of our community. It is through their tireless activism, strength and indestructibility that I am able to be so public about my journey.

CONTENTS

Nevo, dressed as a pirate for Purim, approximately four years old (2000)

Chapter 1
Pretty (Pained) in Pink

There's something quite ironic about writing a life story at my age. I am only twenty after all.

My story begins before I was born.

My mother had a life of travelling and fun interspersed with studying and working as a teacher. But at a certain age, she said, she felt that her biological clock was ringing, and she decided to settle down and take things slower (though most people who know her would say slowing down is not in my mother's vocabulary). At thirty, she met my father and they married. My dad already had three children from a previous marriage but it was important to my mum to have a child. They had some complications while trying to conceive so had to go through IVF treatment. In my mum's words, "Each menstruation brought grief and mourning." Eventually, on the third try, she conceived.

My mum was desperate to have a daughter. She knew due to the fertility issues they had, she would likely have only one child. She prayed for a girl. When asking people whether they would like their baby to be a boy or a girl the usual answer is, "I don't mind as long as it's healthy," but that was not my mum's response. She had picked out only girls' names and was certain of the fact. I often joke with her that her desperation to have a daughter resulted in my trans identity.

Apparently, the moment I was born, she anxiously asked her mother, "Well, what is it?" To which my grandmother replied, "It's a boy!" My mum was horrified, but the doctor quickly interjected and explained I was indeed a girl. My mum was relieved. I wish I could have spoken on behalf of myself then and there; I could have avoided a lot of issues down the track.

I was born into a Jewish family, consisting of a mother (thirty-eight), father (forty-two), half-brother (thirteen), other half-brother (twelve) and half-sister (ten). My dad is Israeli and my mum was born in Australia. Her parents were Holocaust survivors from Eastern Europe who immigrated to Australia during the war.

* * *

I was a confident and outspoken child. I would put on performances for my parents and their friends. A friend of my mother's once told her I would either end up as prime minister of Australia, or in jail – the jury's still out on that one.

It is commonly thought that children are aware of their own gender from about the age of three. At age four I was set on the fact I was a boy. I refused to go to the girl's section at department stores and would only wear clothing designated for boys. Whenever people referred to me as a girl, I would quickly correct them. This led to a few funny instances of strangers asking my gender and my father and me arguing about it. Once, when accused of being a drama queen, my retort was, "I'm a drama *king*."

My mum was upset about all of this, as she had desperately wanted a girl, and to her that involved a certain level of femininity. She wished I would wear dresses and she hated the clothing I insisted on wearing. I liked anything with dragons, skulls or fire. Mum tried to set boundaries as to how masculine I could be. She didn't allow me to cut my hair too short and when she left the room I would instruct the hairdresser to keep cutting. She was saddened by my choices to wear suits in preference to a dress. My dad thought it was entertaining and encouraged me to wear whatever I wanted.

People were not always comfortable with my free expression. At the age of about five, a family friend invited me to her mermaid-themed birthday party. I was not interested in wearing a blue bikini like the rest of the girls; I went as a pirate. I also remember going to synagogue occasionally with my grandma and wearing a suit and kippah (the traditional Jewish head covering – historically worn by boys) and the rabbi was very uncomfortable with it.

At one stage, my mum was coming home from a holiday and I went to the airport wearing a dress. I knew that despite how miserable it would make me, she would be incredibly happy and surprised; and she was. Even at a very young age I learned to compromise my own happiness to fulfil my parents' expectations. Later in life when I tried to conform to femininity to fit in, I could see how happy it made my mother, despite the fact that I was lying to myself.

When I was about seven or eight, my mum and I used to go to a family friend's swimming pool. I wore board shorts and swam shirtless and spent a lot of time constructing games to play by myself. One day, our friend decided I was too old to swim with my shirt off, and my mum told me I would have to start wearing a shirt. I was devastated. I didn't understand why I couldn't continue to be topless like my male friends, or brothers, or my dad. They were older than me but they were still allowed to expose their chests. My mum explained I was growing breasts, something I hadn't been aware of until that moment. I was suddenly acutely aware of my chest in a way I hadn't been before and felt the need to hide it. I felt embarrassed, ashamed and self-conscious. I wore a shirt from then on.

* * *

I had a lot of struggles in my early childhood. I began my education at a private Jewish school where my mother was a teacher at the secondary campus. Boys dominated my year level (as is usually the case in broader society), and I found myself drawn to hanging out with them over the girls. I remember some boys were quite aggressive towards me. I was bullied a lot for being a "tomboy" and also for my weight. I was a chubby little kid and the other kids at school often reminded me of this. These kids already had such ingrained fatphobia and misogyny. In order to fit in, I bullied other kids and that led to a lot of social issues and total loneliness. I wasn't sure how to interact with others. I really struggled to make friends and I spent a lot of time on my own.

One time, my mum and dad went on a holiday for six weeks and left me with my grandma. My mum sent messages to the parents of the kids in my class, explaining the situation and encouraging them to make as many play dates with me as they could while my parents were away. Not one person arranged a thing. I remember the effect this had on me and I still feel the pain. I can't imagine I would have been the nicest person to hang out with anyway because I was so angry all the time, but I didn't know how else to be. I wasn't receiving the support I needed. I saw a psychologist because my parents were concerned about my social issues and the fact that I was presenting as male, but I don't remember getting comfort or support from it, rather feeling like there was something wrong with me. I felt incredibly lonely most of my childhood.

* * *

All of the difficulties I was experiencing were magnified when I got older and moved campuses. The new campus was huge. I was lost and afraid and alone – miserable, with no real friends. A lot of the boys told me I couldn't play with them any more and there was also the presence of older, more intimidating kids. The girls in the years above gushed over how cute the girls in my year were, but they never spoke to me and I felt invisible. I spent most of my lunchtimes walking around the oval on my own or pretending I was sick so I could visit the school nurse. I went there almost every day in the hope I would see my mum and be able to cry to her.

The one time I felt accepted was when a boy in my class and I were playing with the desks and one landed directly on my toe. I ended up in a wheelchair for the rest of the afternoon and everyone was nice to me. For that afternoon, it felt like things could get better. My class made me a card and when I came back to school, I was actually happy to be there.

It didn't last long.

By the end of Year Three, I was truly miserable. The transition to the larger campus had been too hard. Like most kids, it was difficult for me to understand what I wanted and needed. I knew on some level I needed to move schools, but I didn't see that it was a realistic option. While I was trying to figure out how to approach the subject with my mum, she was struggling with how to approach it with me. The school had retrenched a number of teachers, my mother included. This meant I'd have to move schools because we would no longer be receiving the discounted school fees and couldn't afford to pay them at full cost. When my mum told me, I cried, because I couldn't have been happier.

I was to have a trial day at my new school, and Mum set up a play date beforehand with Leila, a girl the same age as me, who she knew through friends. I had never gotten along well with girls but I was desperate to have a new friend, or really, any friend at all. Leila was loud and extroverted. I wasn't sure exactly how to interact with her, but I tried my hardest to be nice. We played computer games and chatted. Years later I found out that the whole time she thought I was a boy and had a bit of a crush on me. I look back on this day as marking the beginning of a huge change in the direction of my life.

I had my trial day during the last term of the year. I was nervous. I entered the unfamiliar territory of a public school around the corner from my house. I had little experience of interacting with anyone outside of the very insular Jewish community and had no idea what to expect. All I knew was I was terrified – terrified of the unknown, of being alone and of being bullied.

The class I joined were decorating rocks. I kept to myself and engaged in the activity. Soon Leila grabbed my arm and pulled me over to her table with her friends. She introduced me to each of them, though the one that particularly stood out to me was Shannon. A tiny, energetic pocket rocket, Shannon immediately started talking to me and asking me questions. This was a pivotal moment for me and I will never forget it. No one had ever been excited to be my friend. I later met Siobhan and the four of us – Leila, Siobhan, Shannon and I – formed a friendship group that would become the main support network in my life. Years later it remains to be that.

* * *

In Year Four, I officially moved to my new school. I was excited and anxious, ready to leave behind my past and the people that had treated me badly. I wanted to start anew, with newfound friends. However, it wasn't as easy to transcend my old life as I had hoped. I still had a lot of misplaced anger and aggression and didn't know how to navigate it or what to do with it. I continued to interact with others in antagonistic ways and isolated myself from the social groups at school. Eventually, Shannon pulled me aside and said, "Listen, I've spent a long time earning my reputation here and you're ruining it. If you want to continue to be my friend you're going to have to get your act together." That was one of the most important conversations of my life. I realised I had people who cared about me, and the way I behaved. What Shannon said made me feel loved, and this helped me take apart the anger I had been holding onto for so long.

Although it still took time, I worked through a lot of that anger and identified that if I wanted to maintain the most important and healthiest relationships I had ever had, I needed to behave more respectfully. For the first time this change was possible, because I felt I had people who supported me.

During this period, I was desperately afraid of not fitting in with the other girls. They invited me to a surprise party they were organising for another friend. I decided that my best bet for fitting in would be to present as femininely as I could. I wore heels, a dress and make-up. I showed up to the party eager to display what I was capable of disguising myself as. Then I realised no one else was dressed like I was and I felt awkward the entire night. It took a while experimenting with different looks and styles to realise the girls actually didn't care what I looked like, they just cared about me. The more I tried to conform, the less I fitted in. The only thing the girls had in common was that they were each unique, powerful and strong, and they loved each other. When I stopped trying so hard to be something I wasn't and allowed myself to be who I was, it was a relief. The only way I could last in this group was by embracing myself. So I did.

Though I know now there was a lot I didn't understand at that time about my identity, at this new school I began the process of understanding who I was. After leaving my previous school, which left me quite broken, I couldn't see what my redeeming qualities were. I had a significant amount of self-loathing. The girls took me in and taught me what was great about me.

* * *

It was radical for me to be part of a group of powerful girls. Up until this point, I had mostly spent time with boys and I had developed a strong sense of internalised misogyny. I saw the feminine parts of myself as lesser. To meet a group of confident girls who taught me I could be myself, and be proud, was revolutionary. This was a period in my life where I strongly identified as female, and a very proud one at that.

This was a time when we all thrived. Looking back now, I can't remember actually sitting in classes. I can only remember the adventures and conversations and things we learned together. We would sit outside the classrooms referred to as the "portables", gossiping on the picnic tables, watching people pass by. For a few years, I truly felt on top of the world. In my mind at least, we were the popular kids. Our friendship group was exclusive and secured. We set a trend in the school, where we wore our school dresses with the school pants underneath. It looked silly, but we loved it and it soon spread around the school. It was a big deal for me to be able to wear a dress with pants underneath and not feel out of place. As a child I would only ever wear dresses with shorts under, so for this to become the norm in the school was quite significant.

This too was the place where I had my first boyfriend. I was in Year Five, in "love" and ready to settle into the kind of glamorous and glorified relationship that had been spewed to me in film after television show after melancholy heartbreak song. I was ready. The boy was in the year above me and I told him I had a crush on him. The relationship lasted about a month, as most true loves in Year Five do, and we went our separate ways.

Nevo with their father, approximately four years old (2000)

Chapter 2
The only constant is change

So much in my life has changed, it is the one thing I can rely on. Things will always change. It is important to explain different parts of my childhood in order to understand how I was shaped as a person, and how I evolved. So the following parts may seem disjointed, but stick with me, because it will help you understand who I am as a person.

* * *

Growing up with much older siblings was difficult. They already had established relationships and I felt like I was an add-on. I was never really sure of what my place was within the family. My siblings were not always nice to me. Whenever we would get together for a Friday night dinner it seemed they had a competition to see who could make me cry first. I left the table many times in tears. I felt ganged-up on throughout my childhood. I think in part this may have been because of the significant age gap.

However, I also think there was an aspect of resentment that my siblings held against me. When they were born, my father was not as established in his career and had to work much harder to provide for them. I think they felt I had a much more privileged upbringing than what they experienced. They all went to public schools and saw my attendance at a private Jewish school as a sign of me being spoiled. From a young age, I tried to be aware of the opportunities I was afforded that they weren't, but I was often spoken over, patronised and taught that until I had more life experiences, my opinion was not valid. I felt like anything I said to them was wrong. They didn't care much about my presentation as a boy, and never really commented, but I didn't feel supported by them. I recall telling my brother about the bullying I was experiencing and how miserable I was, and his response was, "There are kids dying in Africa, you have no idea how good you have it." Because I wasn't particularly close with my siblings, I learned to rely on and enjoy my own company. I had an active imagination and escaped into my own created realities.

One of my biggest secrets was that I loved to play with Barbies. I was embarrassed because they were so girly. I escaped from some of the difficulties in my life by creating my own intricate world of invented characters. It wasn't a reality without its own challenges. I had divorced couples, cheating spouses; I even had a brother and sister that had escaped genocide.

A few times, my dog got into my collection and ripped apart some of my dolls. Once I had appropriately mourned their loss, I developed storylines around how they had died. I was very self-conscious about people watching me play. It was a deeply personal activity and I needed to do it alone. Although this world was nowhere near perfect, it was entirely mine and I felt important.

I escaped into the narratives of my dolls because it was easier to face than what was going on in my real world. Although social issues at my new school were beginning to resolve, I was struggling at home. My parents were fighting a lot and I wasn't sure how to deal with it. I would see my mum cry and try to comfort her. I tended to take her side. I learned from a young age that crying is a sign of weakness. So when my parents fought and I saw one crying, I resolved that this was the place my support was most needed. Over time, I've learned that tears can be a sign of strength and I know now how strong my mother is. But I remember as a child trying to hide my tears. Overflowing with emotion and anger until tears poured out, incriminating me, labelling me as some sort of vulnerable weakling.

I remember countless times, running into my room, trying to hide the shame.

I have also learned that a lack of tears does not necessarily mean a lack of emotion, and that just because I never saw my dad cry doesn't mean he wasn't feeling the same pain as my mum. I've had to think about this a lot because testosterone has now left me far less capable of crying. I love crying, but I can't as often or as much as I feel the need to.

* * *

Another important escape for me was the youth movement I attended. Youth movements are a big part of the Jewish community. There are quite a few, all with varying ideologies and relationships to religion. It's hard to explain what these groups are like to people who have never experienced them for themselves, but a large part is the environment they create in which children have the space to explore issues in the world critically, and actually be listened to. When I was young, my mum sent me to Habonim Dror (Habo). It was the same youth movement she had attended and been a leader in. I was eight years old and beyond excited for my first meeting, even though I didn't know anyone and wasn't sure what to expect. I saw it as an opportunity to start fresh and make friends. A lot of the kids knew each other from school and I wasn't sure how to fit in. I felt out of it for most of my time in the movement. I was different from other kids. I wasn't picked on, but I was mostly ignored. I preferred to be invisible than bullied. I spent a lot of time with the leaders.

I had never interacted with people in their twenties before. These youth leaders were volunteering their time and energy to be educators, and also to provide support and respect for children who wanted to feel heard. Suddenly my opinions were valued and I wasn't told that I didn't know what I was talking about because I was too young.

I owe a lot to this unbelievable place. Every week, I knew there was a safe space waiting for me and people who wanted to see me. I learned how to interpret the world around me and why it's important to be an activist and educator. My motivation to be a role model can be traced back to my early days in this movement. It made me a better person and I am so lucky for that. When everything else changed around me, Habo was the constant in my life.

* * *

Another large part of my childhood was music. I come from a musical family: my sister plays piano and drums, my brother is a rapper and my eldest brother is a pianist. I remember him trying to teach me piano and telling me

I had to practise every day. I went to my mum and said, "What does he think? I can't practise piano every single day! I have a life!" I was six.

When I was about seven years old, my family went to my uncle's house for dinner. I found an old, rusted trumpet and picked it up to see if I could make a sound. An overwhelmingly loud and obnoxious noise filled the air. I loved it. I begged my mum to let me have trumpet lessons at school. She refused. She tried to convince me it would be more practical to learn guitar or something that I could take with me on Habo camps, something to sing with around the camp fire. But I didn't want that. I got such a rush from playing the trumpet that I wanted to see what I could do with it.

Eventually, she gave in and let me have a trial lesson. I walked the long corridors of my school until I found the trumpet teacher's room. He explained to me that most people's lips aren't developed enough to make a sound from a trumpet until they're at least ten years old and was quite impressed that I could. I loved the idea that not everyone could pick up a trumpet and be able to play it. I felt like it gave me a purpose.

My brother and I used to play together a lot. He taught me how to jam and improvise and he even organised a lesson with a friend of his who was in a band that I was a huge fan of. The condition of the lesson was I had to practise for at least half an hour every day for thirty days straight. I kept a journal to record my practising and eventually I got my lesson.

I went on to teach myself guitar many years after my mum had tried to convince me to. Mostly because I was writing my own music and wanted an instrument I could play to accompany my singing. My eldest brother was a huge inspiration for me in my music writing. He supported me and helped me and I looked up to him because of his musical skills and talents. He was the one person who gave my music dedicated time and appreciation.

One of my first very strong musical influences was Missy Higgins. The fact her look wasn't necessarily traditionally feminine was huge for me. I have a strong connection to her music and am a big fan. A lot of the music I have written has been influenced by her style of songwriting.

Another musical influence was P!nk. She was my first exposure to a woman who was comfortable with her own masculinity: powerful and outspoken. Her music helped me get through a lot of hard times. I saw myself in her – saw who I wanted to be – and I developed a deep connection with her lyrics. Her early music addressed the invisibility I felt as a child and showed me that my feelings and opinions were not invalid because of my age. I felt like she understood and heard me and gave me a voice. Her music was a comfort, particularly through the time when my parents were having issues. I am grateful for the effect she had on my life. She taught me to be my own hero, to save myself and that if I want a role model, I may have to be my own.

More recently, the body of work created by Peaches has inspired me. She is a powerhouse of knowledge of gender and sexuality.

* * *

When I was younger I had a few aspirations for my future. I wanted my first job to be as a lolly-maker in a lolly shop. I had plans to be an eccentric scientist, veterinarian or astronaut. When I realised these may not be the most realistic of dreams, I decided I wanted to be a famous actor. After my mum finished work at my previous school, she took over a drama school from her friend and ran after-school drama classes. My mum and I are both quite theatrical, and I felt comfortable expressing myself through acting.

I went on to compete in drama competitions. I put pressure on my mum to find me an agent. She was never that passionate about it, so eventually I took things into my own hands. I found an agent. He told me he had to take headshots of me in order to get me jobs. He was located in Queensland and luckily we had a holiday house there, which was my great-grandmother's old apartment. When we went up for a holiday, I got my headshots. I found the whole experience unbearable. I had no idea how to "model", and at the end of the shoot he said to me, "I'm not going to tell you to lose weight, but I'll tell you not to gain any more." Thank you for contributing to my life-long battle with body negativity!

Nevo, approximately six years old (2002)

CHAPTER 3
Misogyny for Beginners

Naturally, as young girls in a patriarchal society, my group of friends experienced misogyny. It was everywhere: in the media, at school, in our day-to-day lives. Unfortunately, misogyny is one of those things that shows up constantly. Don't worry, if it doesn't come from others, it'll be so ingrained in your own view of the world your internalised misogyny will take over for any misogyny you're missing out on, as if there's some patriarchal quota.

There was an atmosphere all of us felt at school, of having to overcompensate as females in order to be addressed in the same way as the male students. Leila told me she felt she always had to be louder, pretend to be sure of herself, even when she wasn't, to be taken more seriously. We would both get angry when teachers asked boys to help them lift things, when between Leila and myself, we were stronger than all of them put together. There were always boys who had crushes on Shannon, announcing it and subsequently expecting things from her. Teachers made inappropriate comments about our appearances. Leila recalls being told by the art teacher (in relation to her arm hair) that her arms made her look like a monkey. One teacher pointed out my chubbiness often and made comments constantly about my unkempt, curly hair. It resulted in a lot of insecurity.

Leila developed the fastest of our group and was often victim to harassment on the street – badgering from men and catcalling. For a long time I blamed her. We all did. In a lot of ways, she was the girl I never was. She was confident, body positive, sex positive, deeply intelligent and articulate. She didn't care about others' impressions of her. I was constantly embarrassed by her eccentricity and lack of care. I realise now it was less embarrassment and more envy. The internalised misogyny I held closely to myself was often projected on to Leila. I felt she exaggerated her period pains to get attention and I had little sympathy for her when men would gawk and stare. I figured she had brought it on herself.

When she would come to us, distressed about a comment made on the street, or someone physically harassing her, I told her she shouldn't have dressed the way she did. She shouldn't have invited the comments. What did she expect when she had such large breasts? It was the price she had to pay. Anyway, she liked the attention, what was she complaining about? I wished men would look at me that way. I believed all of this, until one particular encounter. Leila was walking home from the train station one day. She was wearing her school dress, so was clearly under-age. A forty-year-old man was staring at her. She felt uneasy and looked away from him, and then he yelled out, "Nice tits." She was probably eleven years old. That was the moment I knew it wasn't her fault; she had done absolutely nothing. She was only trying to get home.

Growing up in a society that teaches women we are only as valuable as our appearance leaves many of us desperately needing validation. I didn't feel valuable because men didn't toot and catcall me. That's how deeply misogyny was ingrained in me. I found myself wanting to be objectified in order to feel attractive. This is what I was shown day in and day out – through the media, parents, family, friends. At school I was policed on how short my dress was, taught not to go out on the street late at night, taught how not to be sexually assaulted. Very rarely have I heard that conversation conducted with my male friends. Very rarely are they taught how not to sexually assault, how to value women for more than the length of their legs, how not to blame women for being distracting by merely having flesh. Taught how to take responsibility for their own actions and thoughts and desires. Not all men sexually harass, but all men need to be taught not to.

* * *

I'm going to talk about periods. I don't care if it causes you discomfort because I can guarantee that it's a lot less uncomfortable than actually having a period.

Unlike a lot of trans people – or at least the ones I have spoken to – my period was not a distressing, traumatising or even upsetting experience. It was an inconvenience and one that I embraced. To be honest, sometimes I even miss it. My girlfriends and I had a tradition that after each person in the group's first period, we would have a little period party and give each other gifts. It was fantastic. Truly counter to what we were mostly taught about periods, which was that they were unsanitary, dirty and a taboo topic for conversation. Certainly nothing to be celebrated. Sanitary item advertisements very rarely even mention the word "period". The portrayal of women with their period is women who don't seem to have their period; happily frolicking around town in white pants without fear. I don't know about you but I am incapable of wearing white pants regardless of whatever sanitary item I may be using. A tampon does not protect me from myself, a notorious food dropper.

In case you haven't noticed, these ads are lies. There is nothing about a period that is white. Periods are red. They're bloody. They're messy. They leave stains and they leak and they make themselves known. When having their period, people don't appear happy and calm as they do in advertisements. They're in a war zone. They're probably angry and in pain. Their body is bleeding out and repairing itself and preparing for a new month. That is hardcore!

For me, my period was a symbol of strength and mindfulness. It was a time of the month where I had only to focus on my needs, both physical and mental. And the fact that we often dismiss people's emotions when they have their period is ridiculous. If anything we should validate their feelings even more, because chances are they have a much heightened awareness of what their needs are at that time. I would also like to point out that there are lots of women who do not have a period, and it certainly does not make them any less of a woman. We have associated periods with womanhood, but this is an incorrect association. There are people of all genders that have periods, and people of all genders that do not.

Leila was the first of our group to get her period. We were all confused, awkward and secretly jealous. We celebrated her period, though she says she felt alone at the time. She was confused that her body was developing faster than her best friends. When Leila got her first bra, I tried desperately to persuade my mum to get me one too. She explained I didn't need one as my chest hadn't developed enough. I tried to convince her by jumping around the house to show how much my breasts would bounce. They didn't, but she let me get a crop top as a compromise.

* * *

At the end of Year Five, my family and I went on a trip to Israel. For the most part it was fantastic. I remember long car drives, beautiful Hebrew music, practising my own Hebrew, my eldest brother writing flashcards (mostly so he could learn Hebrew profanities), unbelievable food and views, and getting to meet my Israeli family.

One night, my parents were having an argument about something and I decided I would try to mediate. I sat with them, asking each for their perspective and attempting to sort through their issues. Not the typical responsibility of a ten year old. It resulted in a huge blow-up with my parents screaming at each other, then me, and then at each other again. Eventually, I ran out of the room in tears. I went next door to where my siblings had congregated.

I didn't have a close relationship with my siblings at that point. They were all at least ten years older than me and at very different stages of life. They comforted me and told me if my parents got a divorce they would support me and be there for me. They told me about my father's divorce from their mother and how they coped. It was the first time I felt genuinely close to them and, to be honest, loved by them. They made it clear I would always be part of the family – something I didn't always feel growing up. I was certain my parents would get a divorce, but they stayed together for another three years.

* * *

Making the decision about which high school to go to was a daunting one. I sat for scholarships at various schools, but I was afraid to approach the private Jewish school world after the experience I had in primary school.

I would be separated from the people who had become my safe place. Shannon would be attending another Jewish school, different to the one I was looking at, and Leila was moving to a girl's school. Siobhan was coming to my new school with me, which was fantastic, but our relationship individually was not yet strong and we didn't feel like we could turn to each other for support. I was worried I wouldn't fit in and would be bullied again. I was also worried I wouldn't be able to control my anger again and would revert to being a bully.

I eventually found a few people I could get along with – all girls – and we developed a friendship. The school I went to was small: around sixty kids per year level and the social dynamics were not easily changed. But I found those I felt comfortable with and we got along quite well.

For my first school camp at my new Jewish high school, I was placed in a cabin with a group of popular girls that I was intimidated by and, up until then, had stayed away from. There were many underlying passive aggressions that could easily be dismissed as being paranoid or misreading the situation. This is how mean people function for the most part. The meanness is so subtle that you begin to question yourself.

On the first day I was in the cabin, a spider appeared and everyone ran out screaming. I didn't understand what was going on, and just wandered out. I was looked at with such judgement that by the next day, when there was another spider in the cabin, I was the first one running out and screaming. I realised I would never fit in with this group of people if I presented in a masculine way. Once again, I tried to conform to femininity to make friends.

* * *

School swimming was really difficult for me. In my early years of school, we were made to get changed in the swimming pool area in front of everyone. I was always self-conscious. I loathed taking my clothes off in front of the other kids. I was able to blend in with the other boys until it came to taking my clothes off. It was in those moments that I was aware of how different I was to the other girls. I hated that I had to wear a one-piece bathing suit, I just wanted to be like the other boys. This experience became one of the first ingredients in a recipe for lifelong dysphoria.

The first swimming lesson we had in high school, I was nervous. I felt more at ease blending in with the girls than I had before, and so I wasn't as paranoid about getting changed. I also had the luxury of changing in a cubicle. But as I sat in my one-piece on the benches, waiting to get into the pool, the girl next to me looked at my legs and said, "Wow, how are you not wearing board shorts? I get so insecure about my legs, I can't deal with my thighs being exposed." She was admiring my confidence and I think identifying that we had similar body types. She was extending some loving solidarity for a fellow fat girl in bathers. However, at this time, I saw being fat as a bad thing and rejected any idea that I could be fat. To be compared with her and admired for my confidence was an insult to me. I was deeply offended and became aware again of my size and weight. For every swimming lesson from then on, I wore shorts.

* * *

I've had a difficult relationship with my body as a woman, as a transgender person, as a non-binary person and simply as a human. I was a chubby kid and I was constantly reminded of it. Much of my childhood was inhibited because of insecurities relating to my body. There is nothing inherently wrong with being overweight, but it has taken me a long time to learn that. My understanding of beauty has been poisoned by rigid societal standards, which has not included being fat. People told me I had a pretty face, that if I lost weight I could be beautiful. I was complimented whenever I did lose weight. Whether it was the result of healthy exercise or being ill and not eating for a few days, that didn't seem to matter, what was important was there was less of me.

As a woman, I became aware I was entitled to less space than men, and I think this was expressed literally through the policing of my body. I was treated differently depending on my size. When I was bigger, people watched me eat. They monitored what food I chose to consume and what clothing I decided to wear. Once I lost weight, people stopped caring, because I was deemed worthy of privacy again.

It is not for anyone else to decide what healthy choices are for me. I refuse to be reduced to just a body. I am so much more than size.

According to my sixteen-year-old self:

"I think that when you stop obsessing about who you are and what people think of you, you're free. I mean, I remember I constantly used to walk down the street, and I was very self-conscious about my weight because I used to be bullied about it. And I'd be pulling out my shirt, playing with it, making sure that none of my fat was showing, and it just held me back from so many things because I wouldn't go on a trampoline; I wouldn't do things like that. Even though it seems small, it was really significant. I missed out on opportunities because of how insecure I was."

There were times when Mum and I were both focused on losing weight and we would compare our weights with each other. It was like some sort of unhealthy, fatphobic competition. We would catch each other out while eating something we had deemed to be banned and would try to push each other in weight loss in all the wrong ways. We weren't focused on being healthy or happy, we were too distracted by the numbers on the scales. A lot of people commented on our weight loss and it perpetuated the dangerous cycle, because we needed that validation. Whenever I was in a situation when I couldn't exercise for a while, I would feel immense self-hatred and disconnection from my body. Often the disassociation I had with my body due to gender issues was masked under this deep insecurity about my weight.

I grew up in a body-negative environment. There's

often this paradox in the Jewish community of feeding your children as much as you can and then shaming them for their weight. That's what my grandparents did. My grandfather would attempt to buy my love with material goods and sugar, and my grandmother spent a lot of my childhood commenting on my weight. She blamed my mother for me being overweight and would frequently discuss it in front of me.

I would suffer intense anxiety about buying new clothes. I hated how clothes looked on me and I despised having to stare at myself in the mirror. Once Mum and I went shopping together and we were trying on clothes in the same cubicle. I took my pants off and she looked down at my legs and said, "Wow, your legs have gotten really big. I hadn't noticed." I immediately covered them up and left the change room. I still have anxiety when trying on new clothes. This is a big reason why I go to second-hand stores to buy my clothing. The sizing charts do not exist and I can mostly avoid divided "Men's" and "Women's" sections.

Having a personal trainer for a brother was both empowering and debilitating. Sometimes he would police my eating, deciding that it was too much "for my age" or "for a girl". Even if there was truth to those words, unsolicited policing of my eating resulted in a lot of anxiety and paranoia. This also occurred often with girls at school commenting on the lunches each other were eating.

At the same time, my brother helped teach me that I was in charge of my own body. If I wanted to change something, I had the power to. I started training with him and after much blood, sweat and tears I felt stronger than I ever had before, physically and mentally.

This situation is still such a point of tension. While I want to thank him for teaching me these lessons, I question whether the cost was worth it. I'm sure there could have been ways to inspire me without having to shut down my eating choices or denigrate my appearance.

I have constantly struggled to have a healthy relationship with exercise. To shift my mind from focusing on losing weight, or even gaining muscle, to exercising for happiness. To have the feeling of accomplishment and the ability to see the lengths to which my body can go and to be reminded that I am alive and well and capable of doing incredible things physically.

Nevo, age twelve, at their bat mitzvah with their sister (2008)

CHAPTER 4
WRONGS OF PASSAGE

In the Jewish religion, when a girl turns twelve and a boy turns thirteen, they are considered Jewish adults and undergo a process of learning for usually a year and then have a coming-of-age ceremony called a bar mitzvah/bat mitzvah, followed by a party. Sometimes this is a spiritual experience, sometimes fun, or sometimes it provides the opportunity to show the rest of the community how much money your family has by holding the most over-the-top party possible.

I got my first period the week before my bat mitzvah and I saw it as a sign that I was truly becoming a woman. My period made me physically a woman and my bat mitzvah would make me a Jewish woman. I did my bat mitzvah classes with a fairly religious synagogue. Through this synagogue, boys had a ceremony in which they read from the Torah and spent a long time learning the passages they would read, while the girls were not allowed to read from the Torah and, instead, performed a play and recited speeches. This is different in the more reform and modern streams of Judaism.

My dad never wanted me to have a bat mitzvah. He didn't understand why I felt the need to, particularly through a religious synagogue. It was important to me at the time. I think I needed to learn what I didn't agree with in order to understand what I did.

I spent a year learning how to be a good Jewish woman. This learning followed the religious laws, therefore "good" was supplementary for "religious" Jewish woman, which I was never going to be – regardless of gender transition. I was controversial in my class, bringing up issues related to animal rights, respect for other religions and contesting the religion's condemnation of homosexuality. My teacher and I argued a lot. I didn't get along with the other girls in the class. They all sat quietly and listened to what we were being taught, while I wanted justification and explanation. "Because God said" wasn't a good enough reason for me. I got to the end of my year of learning and I was apparently ready to be a good Jewish woman. We had the ceremony, which was followed by Israeli dancing and lots of food.

A few months later I had my party. My best friends surprised me and organised a white limousine to pick me up with all of them inside. As a twelve year old this was my dream. The party itself was held in an old recording studio decked out with records all over the walls. I had a DJ and had organised some games to play, some of them a mere ploy to create an environment where I could kiss a crush of mine. Sadly, he considered himself too old for the games and sat out. My brother and I had spent a few weeks writing a song specifically for the bat mitzvah and we performed it on stage together. I sang and played trumpet and he played piano. I still remember the lyrics:

"When I was a little girl I dreamed about what I could be,
an astronaut, mad scientist, working in a lolly factory
Now that I've grown older and I see what I've become,
No matter what the future brings I know it will be fun ..."

True lyrical genius, I think. It's a real shame we were never given a record deal for that one!

* * *

Soon after my bat mitzvah, Leila came out to our group as bisexual and I reacted badly. I told her she was confused and looking for attention. To this day, I am ashamed of myself for reacting that way. I know it affected her.

As a society we have a lot of biphobia. We instil a fear of anyone who doesn't fit into a binary understanding of straight or gay. We view it as a transitional point from one to the other and therefore that it's not valid to identify that way, and it must just be a stage or a way of being greedy. It took me a long time to get out of this mentality. Prompting my defensiveness was that I too felt I maybe wasn't straight and hated that part of myself. It was deeply hidden. I looked at Leila and couldn't believe she was accepting of this sexuality variance and had the confidence to come out.

By the next year, social pressures had settled a bit at high school and I felt more comfortable to be myself. I began thinking more about my own sexuality. I wasn't involved with any of the boys; they were generally too intimidated by me. I wasn't typically attractive, at least by the standards held by the boys at my school. I was chubby and had curly hair and I didn't conform to the traditional beauty norms by straightening my hair or wearing make-up. I wore clothes I liked rather than those boys might find attractive. I felt mostly invisible to them.

I eventually developed an infatuation with a girl in the same year as me that I barely knew. Aside from my eternal love and attraction to P!nk (which I thought was fairly natural as my friends all had a "person they would go gay for"), I'd never had feelings for a woman and this caught me off guard. I wasn't necessarily freaked out by the fact I'd feelings for a girl, I was more concerned about the grandeur of them, and feeling quite obsessive. I wrote my first complete song about her.

I'm not exactly sure how I felt about this discovery. After being biphobic to Leila in her coming out, I didn't know how much of that I was still carrying. I had grown up in an inclusive household with plenty of exposure to sexual variance so I didn't address the feelings that much. At times, I told myself it wasn't a big deal, but I realise now, after having done more unpacking regarding my reaction towards Leila, that maybe I repressed these feelings so I wouldn't have to face them and deal with them. I did discuss my potential bisexuality with some people. The rather strange event of National Coming Out Day (11 October) prompted me to write this to a friend:

"Seeing as how it's National Coming Out Day and all, I wanna fit with the spirit. I think I might be bisexual. I'm not sure and I rlly wont wanna tell ppl or make a big thing but I just wanted to tell you. But I want u to know it doesn't mean anything. Like doesn't mean I'm gonna start being attracted to every girl I know. It's a very rare occasion that I am attracted to a girl our age and it's never anyone I am friends with so don't feel uncomfortable around me cos it's rlly not like that."

I was scared. I felt the need to comfort my friend and assure her I wouldn't be attracted to her but also that I was still partly "normal" and wasn't a "full lesbian". I think I was embarrassed. Particularly because the way I viewed bisexual people was that they couldn't control their sexuality and were constantly on the prowl for anyone. I didn't want to be like that or seen that way. I needed to ensure people wouldn't feel threatened by me. She was good about it, and said she thought I was brave.

* * *

Nevo, thirteen (2009)

When I was fourteen, Mum decided to take me to Israel for a few months to improve my Hebrew before undertaking it as a VCE subject. We would also connect with family and friends as it had been years since our previous visit. We went on an adventure, just the two of us, first staying in San Francisco for a few days with her old leader from Habo. We then went onto New York, which was a mix of trying to keep up with Mum as we strode the streets, conquering as many tourist sites as possible, going to the theatre and eating ridiculous food. There are not many people I know whose ideal travel partner would be their mum, but mine is a walking *Time Out* magazine. Somehow, even in places she's never been, she knows the ins and outs and cool areas to go. New York with her was a dream. Then one night, over the phone, my parents discussed getting a divorce. I sat in the bathroom of the hotel room, crying.

Our time in Israel was both incredible and incredibly rough. I wasn't sure how to cope with my parents getting a divorce. We lived on a kibbutz (communal farm) in the north, where my mum had lived as an eighteen year old. We tried to create a daily routine. I went to school there, and attempted to integrate with the kids on the kibbutz. Unfortunately, most of the kids at the school were not interested in getting to know me and my Hebrew was not of a standard that made communication easy. Breaks and lunchtime were spent keeping to myself and reading books. However, my Hebrew did improve considerably as I interacted with the people on the kibbutz. I spent time with my mum's kibbutz family and became close to her best friend who lived there. Her English was limited and she refused to use it with me anyway, so inevitably I got better at speaking and understanding Hebrew. We lived in Israel for around two-and-a-half months.

When we returned from our adventure, my parents separated. It was something I had expected for a long while and, in fact, often encouraged, but I don't think I was prepared for the displacement I felt as a result. My mum moved out of our family home and went to live with my grandmother until she found her own place. I had never lived with only my dad and everything was unfamiliar and scary. Even the little things I had come to take for granted, like my mum making my lunches before school or cooking meals, were not things my dad was necessarily familiar with. I felt alone in my own house. There was a tangible emptiness. A darkness set upon the place and I no longer recognised the corridors. The home became a house. I spent a lot of time in my room.

My siblings were supportive. They remembered the divorce between their mother and my father and they knew I would be having a rough time. I went into a depression and began to see a psychologist. This was probably my first long depression, and it certainly wasn't my last. Navigating custody and mediation between my parents was challenging – a burden upon me that seemed unfair. I knew things would be better in the long-term but the readjustment took time. The hardest part was that my parents couldn't entirely support me because they were struggling so much themselves. My family was ripped into two and I wasn't sure which side I belonged to.

* * *

On my return to Australia I had planned to shave my hair for The World's Greatest Shave. When I was younger, a close family friend had been diagnosed with leukaemia and it affected me significantly.

In my community, it was quite unheard of for a young girl to shave her head. I got a lot of comments about it, mostly regarding the fact that I would likely regret it, or I should at least lose some weight first, so my face would look better without hair. I was not concerned about any of these things. Besides, high school was not exactly going to be the peak of my attractiveness, so even if I didn't look good, I was willing to compromise for a greater cause. I knew this was something I needed to do.

I organised an event with my friends and family where I could shave my head in front of everyone and make it a community-orientated occasion, and I offered them each the opportunity to cut off one of my plaits. Once my hair was entirely shaved, I felt truly liberated. I felt in control of my appearance and marked the cutting of my hair as entering a new chapter of my life. I shed some of the pain I was feeling and tried to rebuild myself as a new and powerful person. I managed to raise a sizeable amount of money and was proud of myself for organising the entire event on my own. Besides, I think I looked badass with a shaved head!

There's something quite incredible about the Jewish community, and I imagine any small community. Once one person finds out about something, so does the entire community. When I shaved my head, rumours started about me being a lesbian. Despite the fact that people knew I had shaved my hair for a cause, apparently the shorter your hair, the more attracted to women you are. A bald head constitutes a lesbian – rather than actually being attracted to women.

I thought it was amusing and I was excited to be a bald, straight woman, defying stereotypes and embracing my look despite the rumours. And then I realised I was gay.

* * *

There was no light-bulb moment with my sexuality. I didn't wake up one day a gay woman. It was a growing awareness that came to the front of my consciousness when it was supposed to. I was incredibly lucky to attend a school that was part of the Safe Schools Coalition. We were the first Jewish school in Australia to join the coalition and it contributed significantly to my mental health and wellbeing. The year above me had quite a few LGBTQIA+ (Lesbian, Gay, Bisexual, Trans, Queer, Intersex, Agender/Asexual + other identities that may exist in this community) students and they pushed for the school to join and develop a queer support club. I heard of this club at the end of Year Nine when I was fourteen, and went to the first meeting as a "straight supporter". Or, at least, that's what I told my mum.

I lingered in the school corridor while people collected their things and left. I worried they would see me waiting and would know where I was going. I was panicking. I thought about bailing on the meeting. I wasn't sure why exactly I was going; I just knew I needed to. One of the girls from the group noticed me and asked if I was coming to the meeting. I hesitated and followed her into a classroom with frosted windows, so no one could see in. We sat in a circle and went around introducing ourselves and discussing our sexuality. I explained I thought I may be bisexual, but honestly had no idea. I mentioned my mum had always told me if I grew up to be a lesbian she wouldn't be surprised. We had a teacher present as a liaison, who helped us to change any school policy that was potentially discriminatory towards the queer and gender non-conforming students. The school later developed a gender-neutral school uniform for anyone who didn't want to wear either the "male" or "female" uniforms.

The leader of the group looked at me as I explained my sexuality. Throughout the meeting I wasn't sure if she was flirting with me or just being friendly. My heart raced and my palms got sweaty. I was overwhelmingly attracted to her. I had never felt that way about anyone. I couldn't wait for meetings each week. I just wanted to be near her, but I was also terrified. We began speaking more and more; I pretended to be confident and experienced. I had no idea what I was doing. We began messaging a lot over Facebook, eventually via text. I could feel things progressing but I wasn't sure if I was just making it up. One night, she came over for a sleepover so we could do some homework together. I knew we weren't going to do homework. I had never had a sexual interaction with anyone. The furthest I had gone was kissing, and I never particularly enjoyed it. Probably because I was kissing boys I didn't actually like.

We sat on my bed talking. I have no idea what was said. All I could think about was kissing her. Her smell was intoxicating – I can still remember it. I ate some chewing gum and before I knew it, she was kissing me. It was amazing, also unexpected and scary. I didn't want to any more. I told her I needed to go to the bathroom. I spat my gum out in the sink and looked in the mirror. I told myself this is what I wanted, what was I doing? I needed to go back out there. Things escalated further than I was comfortable with. I didn't feel like I could say no, didn't want to offend her or expose myself as inexperienced. I felt pressured, uncomfortable and overwhelmed. When I told her I didn't want to have sex she stopped the kissing, turned around and said we may as well go to sleep then. I apologised and felt terribly guilty.

The next morning she told me things didn't feel right between us. Cuddling me didn't feel like it did with her ex. Was it okay if we were just friends? "Of course it's okay," I said. It wasn't okay. She left. I was devastated. She had made huge hickeys on my neck, as if she felt it necessary to mark her territory. I hated them, and also kind of loved them. They made me feel grown-up, sexually experienced. I tried to hide them throughout the peak of summer by wearing a scarf at school. Everyone noticed. She mostly avoided me in the hallways, while I was dying for her attention. She prided herself on being a player, sleeping with as many people as she could and cheating on them with others. She used me to feel good about herself, while I was falling apart. I begged her to give me a second chance. She told me she wasn't interested, but then when I least expected it, she made out with me. She strung me along for a long time and I didn't know how to protect myself. It was my first heartbreak, and one I will never forget.

My mum eventually saw the hickeys on my neck. I had tried for weeks to hide them from her. She asked if they were from a girl and I couldn't lie to her. She didn't want to hear about it, was visibly uncomfortable and we didn't talk about it for a while.

I wasn't sure that I was a lesbian. I wasn't certain I would never fall in love with a man, or someone who wasn't a woman, and I felt scared that if anything changed, it would invalidate the feelings I was having then. I assured Mum I wasn't a "full lesbian" and that I still liked men. She saw this as a way of holding onto hope that I could possibly marry a man and have children.

Mum had told me for so long she wouldn't be surprised if I turned out to be a lesbian, but she was. I always imagine parents are kind of like GPS – they have set destinations for their children. In the Jewish community that quite often tends to be for their children to become a doctor or lawyer, and if anything sets them off track, it takes a little time to re-route. I think that's what my mum went through when I came out. So I spent time at my dad's house, so she could process things alone.

The whole concept of coming out bothers me. I hate the idea that someone is straight until proven otherwise. This is incredibly harmful to young queer people and other members of marginalised communities. Instead of expecting people to go through a deeply personal and exposing experience of revealing to everyone that they are not what they were assumed to be, we should stop making assumptions about people.

One issue for Mum was that she was no longer sure how to monitor my sleepovers, because suddenly anyone could be a love interest. I had to convince her I wasn't romantically involved with everyone I was interacting with, especially at the age of fourteen.

My friends were understanding about my coming out. I explained I was no longer interested in boys. Some of my friends asked if I was going to become attracted to them, and joked that they would no longer invite me to pool parties, because I would look at them in their bikinis. I told them not to flatter themselves; they weren't my type anyway. The same way they were not attracted to every boy in the world, I wasn't going to like every single girl, especially my friends. Boys in my year level tried to argue with me that lesbian sex isn't real sex, showing me the definition of sexual intercourse in the dictionary as evidence against my identity, despite many of them having a rather large collection of lesbian porn on their computers. I was frustrated that I had to defend myself against their vitriol, and no one was there to argue alongside me.

Through coming out, I began my lifelong vocation of becoming a walking search engine. Something very fascinating happens when people discover you are different to them. They forget other resources exist, and direct all of their questions to you, often without recognising the mental and emotional energy required to educate them.

I waited before coming out to the rest of my family. I went on a holiday with my dad to Vietnam and one night over dinner I kept bringing up gay issues in the media. Eventually, he said to me, "Is there something you'd like to tell me?" So I told him I was gay. His response: "No worries, you're always welcome to bring home a girlfriend to my house, as long as you don't make out with her in front of me, but that would be the same as if you had a boyfriend." And that was that. I was relieved.

My dad told my siblings, which I hadn't exactly given permission for. I think it's important not to come out for someone without their consent, but it did pave the way for me to discuss it with them. They were unsurprised and supportive. However, it was interesting to see the ways in which my brothers' language shifted around talking about my partners. When I was assumed straight, they would make jokes about bashing up my boyfriends. This changed when I started dating girls. They suddenly commended me for dating hot girls and I felt rewarded for being sexual, rather than punished.

Nevo, sixteen, on a camping trip (2012)

Chapter 5
Queerings

Often I've heard "It's just a phase" and "You'll grow out of it" used about me and other queer people in relation to our gender and sexuality. Well, guess what? *Everything* is a phase. Like that person you can't believe you dated in high school, or that TV show you used to love but can't stand any more, or the course you dropped out of, or the friendship that ended over time. It doesn't mean those things weren't important or meaningful when they happened, it only means nothing is permanent and things change. Who would we be if we didn't evolve and grow throughout our lives?

The fear of uncertainty around my sexuality dissipated as I began to recognise there is no true certainty in something that is destined to be fluid. I felt more confident in identifying as a lesbian, but this came with its own internal difficulties. I had to say goodbye to the heteronormative life – a "normal" heterosexual life with a nuclear family – I had been told I would have. Although things are changing, there's still not a lot of representation in the media of non-normative family structures. I had always felt I would be a parent one day so it scared me to be a lesbian. I didn't understand how I could negotiate those two things. I began to mourn the idea of having a husband and kids, and tried to comfort myself in the knowledge that no matter my sexuality, I could still be a wife and mother regardless.

Things have changed significantly since then. I see more representations of families that could suit the future I want to have.

* * *

I met my first girlfriend at a Minus18 event when I was fifteen. Minus18 is a wonderful organisation I've had the privilege of both being a patron at and working with. They run social and dance events for LGBTQIA+ people under the age of twenty-one and I am so grateful I discovered them when I did.

I met Tia at one of their social events and added her on Facebook. We spoke for a while online and then met up and watched a movie. I felt awkward, confused and excited. I had a big crush on her but it became clear she wasn't interested in me in a romantic way. I hoped things would change. I wanted her to be my girlfriend more than anything. She began dating her best friend and I was incredibly jealous. I didn't understand why she couldn't be with me. She came over for a sleepover and we spoke about her relationship. She told me she wasn't monogamous and wasn't interested in being with only one person. I didn't understand at all, but I realised that perhaps her relationship didn't need to be an obstacle to us getting together. I wasn't really sure how to flirt but something must have worked because before I knew it, we were kissing. I had never felt anything like this before. I was overwhelmed and short of breath. Before we went further, she asked if I was comfortable. I wasn't used to that. Consent was never something I was taught in sex-ed classes and it wasn't something I had learned in my previous sexual experience. I was surprised at Tia's diligence in making sure I felt comfortable.

Through Tia, I developed self-confidence. I owe a lot of who I am to her. Together, we learned about feminism and gender politics. I was in a safe relationship, where I could navigate challenging topics and learn.

* * *

It was Year Ten when I first owned my feminism. I had

thought about it before, spoken about it and fought for its politics without realising, but I think this was the point where I truly took on the term for myself.

I'm not going to make you a feminist. I'm not going to waste words trying to convince you. Do your own research, make up your own mind. I am a feminist and I will never apologise for it. Once I began to see the world through a feminist lens, it was difficult to switch it off. I could suddenly see the underlying oppressions and microaggressions of the patriarchy. My awareness of women's issues spread into other intersecting marginalised communities and I was suddenly aware of many things I hadn't recognised earlier.

I found support in Tia and the queer community. However, my fellow students did not appreciate my newfound and passionate feminism. I was already othered for being a lesbian, for shaving my hair when I was younger and for generally not giving a shit about the expectations put on me. I had a bunch of piercings, dyed hair and I wore my uniform the way I wanted to. Needless to say, my school wasn't happy with me, despite the fact that I was an A-grade student. Students, and particularly boys, were intimidated by my opinions. People boxed me in as political, opinionated and radical, and therefore didn't want to hear anything I had to say. I wasn't trying to be political for the sake of it.

There's often this misunderstanding surrounding issues of oppression and privilege that people are being too "politically correct" or politicising something unnecessarily. This statement usually, if not always, comes from someone with immense privilege. It is easy to be cool, calm and collected about an issue that doesn't and hasn't ever affected you. But my life and my body is political. Not necessarily because I wanted them to be, but because they had been politicised, and that made me opinionated and angry. Besides, as Laurel Thatcher Ulrich said, "Well-behaved women seldom make history."

* * *

As I embraced my lesbian identity and a long-repressed masculinity, I found new clothing and new goals for my body. Accepting I was a masculine person who had always been interested in developing large muscles was liberating for me. I stopped seeing my body as impossible. I had always felt uncomfortable in what I had deemed a fat body, but felt I could never truly be skinny like the girls I went to school with, or saw on television, or literally saw everywhere. I tried so hard to lose weight and slim down, and I did, but my body wasn't built that way. I wasn't petite and I was never going to be.

Once I stopped caring about the attention of men, I

no longer cared about the beauty standards they had set. I didn't need to be skinny to feel attractive as a lesbian. I saw a lot of diversity in my community and felt liberated to know I no longer had to try to be something I wasn't. I began to gain muscle – something I had always wanted to do – and wasn't worried any more that I would appear too manly, which I had been concerned about when identifying as straight. My focus in exercise shifted from losing weight to gaining muscle, which made me feel powerful for a long time. I thought this process would help create a better relationship with my body. It did for a while, but there was always a dissonance between how I felt inside and what my reflection showed, and I had always attributed it to my weight. So when that weight reduced and I wasn't feeling any different, there was more confusion about who I really was.

* * *

Habonim Dror was still a huge part of my life. In Year Eleven, members of the movement have the opportunity to become leaders themselves. I was excited to become a leader. For six months prior, I and others in the movement had been part of a process called *Hadracha*. *Hadracha* loosely translates to "leadership". *Lehadrich* is "to lead", and the words stem from their *shoresh*, or "root", which is *derech. Derech* means "pathway". Basically the concept is about not necessarily creating the pathway, but helping kids find it and being there to support them. The idea of the movement is very much a sort of "leading from behind" mentality, for people to discover their own ideas but have leaders behind them, supporting and encouraging their development.

We spoke a lot about the expectations of being a leader in the movement: what it meant to take responsibility for a group of kids and what standards we should be holding ourselves to. I wanted to provide the type of support to children that I had received at the movement when I didn't feel I had it in many other places.

Throughout Year Eleven, I led kids from Year Four. I was part of a group responsible for running weekly informal educational programs as well as biannual camps. The movement took a large chunk of my time and energy. This affected my relationship with Tia as we lived about an hour apart, and weekends were the only time we could spend together. Saturdays became entirely enveloped by Habo commitments. Through Habo however, I felt for the first time I could be a leader. One week, I ran a program on role models. At the end of the program a little girl, probably not older than nine, came up to me and asked if I wanted to know who her role model was. Assuming it would be a celebrity of some sort, I was immediately taken aback when she told me her role model was me. After my childhood of exclusion, isolation and repressed anger, I had been afraid that I could never be a role model to anyone. I had been a bully, I had treated people badly and I didn't think it was possible to be someone people looked up to.

Year Eleven was quite a difficult year overall. I struggled to balance Habo commitments, work, my relationship and studying Year Twelve Hebrew. I broke down many times to my Hebrew teacher, who was my mentor and guiding angel. Her office was always open for rants, tears or a cup of tea. I am grateful to her for giving me the space and understanding to love and believe in myself.

* * *

Nevo and Tia at the Minus18 Same-Sex and Gender Diverse Formal (2012)

Year Twelve began and immediately I felt anxiety and encroaching depression. I am lucky to be capable academically and to have access to the kind of education that I do, but VCE was utterly terrifying. In so many ways, high school is a breeding ground for mental illness. And if *I* felt that way, I can't imagine what it would have been like for people with more issues dealing with academia. School was never too difficult for me – I was always difficult on myself. Nothing I did was ever good enough; I never remembered the good marks, only the bad. I became an overachieving perfectionist.

Luckily for me, across all the mental health issues I was dealing with and the huge workload to keep up with the private school VCE pressure, I discovered gender dysphoria.

Gender dysphoria is this fun thing that happens sometimes when you exist outside of society's very narrow understandings of gender, and it slowly started sneaking into my life. I didn't know what it was at the time, but on a long road trip I began to unravel the signs that maybe something deeper was going on.

Tia and I planned to go to ConFest together. ConFest is a folk festival I had been going to since I was a young child. It involves various workshops on physical, mental and spiritual ideas and provides an environment in which nudity is encouraged and a non-judgemental, free attitude is nurtured. Tia had just gotten her licence and we were excited to get away together, just the two of us. The drive to the festival is six hours. We spoke about everything and after a significant portion of the trip, I felt the need to bring up gender as a conversation. I explained that certain things in our relationship were becoming uncomfortable for me and I was experiencing a lot of sexual anxiety. Something had shifted lately and I was no longer comfortable with the kind of sex we were having. I wasn't sure why but I was finding it distressing.

Tia was amazing. She immediately came up with ideas to improve things. She also tentatively mentioned that I might be transgender. I became defensive. It was something she had brought up before and I had immediately rejected. She backed off but suggested I start doing some research. I tried to push the conversation to the back of my mind until I could return home and get online.

Going to ConFest was always a bit confronting for me. Naked people comfortable in their skin was something I wasn't often exposed to. I was always really uncomfortable in my body, but I hadn't met any women who weren't. Our society profits a lot from people's self-doubt. The more you hate your body, the more money you'll spend on products that promise a solution.

I had never liked being naked and I had never been naked at ConFest. I loved being surrounded by naked strangers in a totally non-sexual situation, but I didn't think it was something I could do myself. The people I went with were encouraging of nakedness and for the first time in a long time I took my shirt off in public. I had such a heightened awareness of my body, of other bodies and of the wind on my nipples. I spent most of the time walking around at ConFest with my breasts out, talking about how they were out. Tia stood next to me, laughing at how much I was talking about the fact I was topless. I was trying to convince myself that this was a liberating experience for me and I was reclaiming my body, but really I was just anxious and trying to ignore the niggling at the back of my brain telling me that this didn't feel right.

When I got home from ConFest, I started researching. Although I had been in the LGBTQIA+ community for a couple of years, I had never been exposed to transgender issues. I think that's because the community is quite divided. Often mainstream discourse from the gay community focuses on its L, G and maybe occasionally B members, but there is a rather large eclipse of the other letters in the acronym. I knew nothing of trans, gender diverse and intersex people.

I looked up the sort of anxieties and concerns I was having: dreams I had where I was almost always a man, and the fact that whenever I played online roleplaying games, I always chose the male character. I'm not saying this is the same for everyone. There is no single trans narrative. This is my experience and my experience alone. But I read things online from other trans people that resonated with me. With each story and anecdote I read that I could relate to, I developed a deep, tight knot in my stomach that I knew would not easily come undone.

* * *

I became obsessed. My dysphoria started to grow and take over. My head was filled with paranoia and self-hatred. I ran away from the world around me that I felt would never understand, into the world of the internet. I went out less and immersed myself deeply in my research every day after school. It was a can of worms that once opened could not be closed, and I found solace in the research that I didn't quite feel in anything or anyone else.

A lot of how I felt as a child started to resurface and I spent time looking back on old photos and trying to understand why it was that I identified as a boy for five years. I had always assumed it was because I was a lesbian and as a child didn't understand that. I thought maybe my younger self felt in order to be attracted to women I would have to be a man. The thing I hadn't considered was that I wasn't attracted to *anyone* when I was four. This had nothing to do with attraction or sexuality. It was about me, internally, not my interactions with others. I had to begin to look at that stage of my life very differently and unpack some of the meaning behind it. I had never thought any of the feelings I held as a child could be relieved in any way, but the more research I did, the more I felt truly seen. Things started to make sense and I wasn't sure if I wanted to celebrate or break down and cry. I felt like I was finding a part of myself that had been lost for a very long time. But did I want to find it? I was scared of this discovery. I didn't know who I was any more.

I desperately searched for information on trans issues. The last few years have brought an increase of transgender representation and topics into the mainstream media. However 2013, although not long ago, had very little discussion surrounding these issues. I wasn't sure where to turn for support. Part of me wanted to run away, deny and reject any potential that I could be trans. I wanted to ignore the feelings that were powerfully bubbling up. But I could think of nothing else.

I needed to get to the truth, because I wasn't sure if I had been lying to myself for my entire life. I couldn't work out which versions of myself had been the most authentic ones. I thought I had been genuinely honest about who I was throughout my life. I was panicked and so deeply trapped in my own head I felt no one else could reach me. I didn't know how to put the feelings and experiences I was having into words. I felt entirely isolated.

I thought finding trans stories would maybe give me the vocabulary to express the mess that was happening in my brain. The only trans representations I managed to find ended in tragedy, heartbreak and death. There was nothing in mainstream media to show me that it was okay to be trans, that I could have a future.

Something scary happened at this point. I stopped imagining myself as an older person. Before this I had spent a lot of time romanticising my future. I would often think about getting married and having kids, what job I would have, my house, my pets, how I would go on to live my life. As soon as I thought that I might be trans, that all came to a dramatic halt. I couldn't see it any more. I couldn't imagine myself surviving this discovery, and if I did, I was unable to grasp the idea I could be happy.

CHAPTER 6
MY MOTHER DOESN'T KNOW MY NAME

I went into survival mode. I got out of bed each day, went to school, kept my head down and came home. My days lost meaning and I was just trying to get through them. I stopped picturing a happy future because I didn't believe it was possible. I had an overwhelming urge to rip out of my body and fly away. I didn't want to be me any more.

I was a hazard to myself; I didn't fit into the world. I couldn't see people like me anywhere, and I was consciously aware of myself all the time. I became fed up with the discussion I was having with myself. I wanted to shut off. It felt as if I had brought this discovery upon myself, when everything had been fine, as if I had some sort of deep desire to ruin everything. I was angry. I hated myself. I wanted to be someone else.

With each day, getting out of bed took more energy. Bags formed under my eyes and my body became heavier. I was lugging around chains of emotional weight. I had dealt with depression before, but this was unlike anything else. I was constantly anxious and quiet, conjuring up scenarios where I would tell people I might be trans and they would never speak to me again, or worse, become violent. I had created a world of my own, filled with misery, and I needed to let someone in before it swallowed me whole.

I hid this from my mum; I didn't think she would understand. At school I performed a false happiness, pretended to be okay so no one would see what was really happening – I was falling apart. I needed to hold myself together by the thinnest string because I could not afford to lose everything at this point. This was my final year of school, I just needed to make it through.

Before things got worse I turned to Tia. She didn't understand what I was going through, but she tried, and I didn't feel as alone. Shannon, Siobhan and Leila were on call. They came over whenever I needed them and sat with me, even when I didn't feel like talking. I didn't tell them what was going on; I didn't need to. I started to see a faint light in the distance. When I finally did tell the girls that I thought I might be trans, Leila looked at me and said, "I know."

* * *

With my friends and partner by my side, I became more stable and was able to face the reality that I was transgender. As much as those closest to me tried their best, they could not truly understand how I was feeling or what I was going through. I needed to immerse myself in the transgender community.

Because I didn't actually know anyone who was transgender, I turned to YouTube and stumbled upon a world I hadn't realised existed – the trans world. There were videos where trans people spoke of their experiences and lives at different ages and stages of transition. The most striking thing was a lot of them looked happy. I started to piece together a future I thought had shattered permanently.

I stumbled upon a "One Year on Testosterone" transition video made by a transgender man. It was a series of photos and short clips, following his life until he had been on testosterone for a year. There were photos of him as a young child, teenager, getting married to a man, presenting as masculine and in a relationship with a woman. Then there was a short video of him explaining he was trans and was about to undergo a medical transition. The photos showed him and his girlfriend, his first testosterone injection, videos of the changes he was experiencing. It was quite surreal and I watched these photos and videos of him changing, with his girlfriend right beside him. Then there was a photo of her pregnant. I burst into tears. I wasn't sure how they managed to have a baby, but all that mattered to me was that it was possible. They got married and there were photos of him holding his child. When I realised I was trans I stopped imagining ever being a parent. This video changed everything. He was happy, healthy and alive, and I could be too.

I was overcome with emotion. I showed my mum the video. Not because I was ready to tell her how I was feeling, but because I needed to share this video with someone. I needed her to respond emotionally and I guess I wanted her to miraculously understand this was going to be my journey too. I told her I had a trans friend and it was important to me that she watches this video, so she will understand better. She watched it while cooking, said, "That's nice," and turned back to her pot. I waited to see if that was the end of her reaction but found comfort that she hadn't been appalled by what I had shown her.

I discovered later she had called a friend of hers immediately after and said, "I have a terrible feeling that my child might want to be a man." We didn't talk about it again for a while. I was feeling confident she would handle my coming out fairly well, while at the same time she was terrified this video was an indication I might be trans.

I came across an interview on YouTube with a trans man and his mum. I had never seen anything like it before. I had assumed most trans people would be estranged from their parents because their family could never come to understand or accept them. At least that was the impression from the tragic media narratives I had been exposed to. The video was of a trans guy only a few years older than me, sitting with his mum and discussing how his transition had been for them. His mum spoke about how it helped both of them that her son had told her about his gender questions early on in his process, before he was more certain of himself. She explained that this offered them the opportunity to go on the journey together and support each other. She felt that questioning his identity alongside him allowed both of them to understand things more deeply and it was empowering for their relationship.

I had initially planned to wait before talking about my gender with my mum, but this video made me rethink things. I thought it could be an opportunity for us to be closer. I realised in my depressive and self-hating state, I was shutting her out and maybe I needed to give her more credit. I resolved to speak to her earlier. We had always been very close and I wanted her to go on this journey with me. I felt alone enough in my own head; I didn't want to feel alone in my house too. I needed her to understand that I was struggling, that it was complex and that I was in need of support.

One day we were driving and I told her I was beginning to question my gender. She immediately freaked out. (I recognise retrospectively that the car is probably not the best place to reveal life-changing realisations.) She explained how much more radical a gender transition is and said she had come to accept my sexuality, "Why can't you be happy with that and not push things further?" She was angry, confused and upset. I felt the same way. I sat there, gently sobbing, holding my breath until we arrived home. I felt sick.

As soon as we got home, I launched out of the car, tears pouring down my face. I raced straight to my room. I exploded – all the anxieties and fears I had been holding onto erupted. Things were only beginning to look up after the deep pit I had fallen into, and in that moment I was right back at the bottom.

I heard Mum's footsteps coming up the staircase. I didn't want to speak to her. I wasn't sure what to say. She came in and I turned away from her. I didn't want her to see how much I was panicking. She wouldn't understand. But she held me and said that no matter what, I would always be her child and she would love and support me regardless. She had never been particularly good at comforting me or understanding what I need when I'm panicked, but what she said calmed me and I appreciated it. She left shortly after and, in the exhaustion I had created through my anxiety, I fell asleep. It seemed the worst was over.

We didn't speak about that day again. I realised we weren't speaking much at all, actually. The tension in our household was tangible. Mum wasn't sure how to process the information I had given her. She went from silent to angry. She lashed out at me because she felt this was something I was purposefully forcing upon her, as if I wasn't content with the difficulties in our life already, and I was trying to make things harder. This made everything worse.

I longed for the invisibility I once had. I felt exposed and vulnerable and attacked. She used aggressive and antagonistic language towards me and to the parts of my body I was feeling anxious about. Home became a scary place for me. I spent more time at friends' places as well as my dad's. I hated myself enough. To see it mirrored even in the slightest way in my mother was too much for me to handle. I needed to escape.

I had very rapidly transitioned from confident and outgoing back to quiet and anxious. I became smaller, took up less space and my head was filled with aggressive words and reactions I expected to hear from everyone around me. My dysphoria spread like a virus through my body. Parts of myself I had never quite been aware of felt like they had grown or pronounced themselves in ways they hadn't before. I had a heightened awareness of the lumps below my shirt, the delicateness of my fingers, the size of my hips, my voice. I hated everything.

* * *

I wanted to go out into public dressed as a man. I wanted to put into practise the feelings I was having and see whether it felt right. I wanted to know if being perceived or "read" as male would alleviate the anxiety I was having.

I started researching binders. A binder is an undergarment that can press your breasts down to make a more flat-looking chest. I had always hated my breasts. They were totally different sizes. I was incredibly insecure about them and hated looking at them. I remember going to the doctor when I was younger and asking if there was anything I could do about it. Instead of telling me how normal it is for breasts to be different sizes, she told me my only option would be surgery. Chest surgery was on my mind from a young age.

I wasn't sure what a binder would feel like, so I was too scared to buy the binders that were available online.

They were expensive and I felt like purchasing one would be a big decision. So Leila and I went to a department store to buy tight crop tops that could do the job. I was excited to see how flat I could make my breasts. The problem was I had to choose a flat chest over breathing.

I wore them for a few days before I almost passed out. But the feeling I got when I looked in the mirror at my flat chest revealed to me that buying a proper binder was an investment I would have to make. I found one online that looked good and ordered it. I had to use Tia's credit card because I was too afraid to ask my mum for hers. I counted the days until its expected delivery.

When it finally arrived I rushed to my room and put it on. It was comfortable and it didn't constrict my breathing to the extent that the crop tops had. I looked in the mirror and couldn't believe what I was seeing. I emptied my cupboard of my favourite shirts and tried them on with my new flat chest. Everything sat better on my body and for the first time I believed I could pass as a boy. I took photos and posted them on a private blog I had created to track my transition. I kept running my hand over the totally unfamiliar flatness.

* * *

When I was born, I was named Liat. Liat is a Hebrew name that my mum felt very strongly about, one that I grew to feel a deep connection with. It translates loosely into English as "You're mine". It was a special message from my mother to me. Those series of letters somehow became defining to who I was as a person.

Some trans people hate their birth names. There is a lot of associated trauma and distress and many refer to it as their "deadname". It is considered an act of transphobia to use someone's birth name without their consent. I have had mine used many times without consultation, in interviews and articles and by people who have decided it is too difficult to adjust to a new name. That name being used as a way of invalidating my identity has caused a bitter rift in my relationship with those people. Though truthfully, I love my birth name. Revealing that name to people is a recognition of closeness. So by choosing to include my birth name at this point in my book, I am allowing you to see a very guarded part of me.

There will always be a part of me that is Liat. I think of her almost as a little sister, and sometimes I miss her. When I refer to my past self, sometimes I use "she" pronouns and sometimes I use my old name. By no means does that give permission to anyone else to do the same. I exclusively use they/them and he/him pronouns now, and that is what I expect people to use when referring to me in the past. I know this sounds confusing, but I think it's okay to have a different set of rules for myself in relation to my gender and past than I do for others.

There is a part of me that wishes I could have kept my birth name. But as time went on, my name felt distant. I started to see it as a "girl's name" rather than my name. Out of the mouths of those I knew would not accept me it felt like a slur, an insult and total invalidation. When people said that I would always remain Liat to them, it felt like they would never see me for who I truly was, just merely the performance I had been. Once my name became my insult, there was no getting it back.

I spent a long time deciding on a name for the new me. It's difficult to choose your own name. I started making lists and searching Hebrew baby-name books. It was important to me that the name would be Hebrew as my Israeli heritage is central to my identity. I thought about Lior – close to my name; maybe too close. It would feel strange correcting people. Also, it's a gender-neutral name and it was very important to me to have a masculine name (whatever that means!). I read my list of new names to Tia. She didn't like any of them. But they were Hebrew and probably sounded very foreign and strange to her. I would have loved my mum to be a part of my name-choosing process, except she was not ready to face the reality of my transition.

I went away for the weekend to a Hebrew camp organised by my school, in which Israeli leaders came to teach us about topics relating to Israel. I asked one of them what her favourite Hebrew boy's name was and she said Nevo. And something about it felt right. I also loved that it could be shortened to Nev for those who couldn't correctly pronounce it. I told my close friends and Tia and I started living more comfortably in myself.

But my mother didn't know my name. I left the house and was Nevo, authentically and truthfully, and at home I was Liat, quiet, sad and hidden. Eventually my mum found out my new first name, and I gave her the opportunity to choose my middle name. That is how I became Nevo Amiel Zisin.

* * *

With the tension with my mum over gender issues, I avoided telling my dad I was trans. Similar to when I came out as a lesbian, I offered myself adjustment time between parent coming outs. We were at lunch when I decided to tell him. I could barely hear conversation over the sound of my thumping heart. It was time.

Dad and I had always had a relationship that might be described more stereotypically as father–son.

We used to wrestle, go fishing and fly kites. Those aren't activities restricted to boys but I told myself becoming his son wouldn't change our relationship very much. At the end of our meal, I quickly blurted out how I had been feeling. He took a moment, looked at me, and said something along the lines of, "I'd be lying if I said I was completely surprised. I will always support you no matter what. I just want my kids to be happy." I couldn't believe the relief that followed. I thought he would understand but I didn't quite expect the degree.

It did however become clear that his initial reaction was perhaps more accommodating than he was feeling. He struggled with the new reality, especially in conversations over medical intervention and he often tried to tell me how supportive he was, in a way that felt to me like he was congratulating himself.

People often tell my parents how incredible they are for supporting me. While this is true, it certainly doesn't make me feel very good about what a "burden" I have been to my parents and how much they've had to "overcome" to accept me. This reinforced the feelings I had that I was consciously bringing this selfish and hugely difficult transition onto my family as a way of being destructive. I had no choice in the matter; this was survival. Believe me, I am grateful for their support, but that doesn't mean I shouldn't have expected it.

Accepting your child for who they are and being there for them, regardless of how difficult it may be, should not be placed on a pedestal.

Leila, Siobhan, Shannon and Nevo at their Year Twelve formal (2013)

Chapter 7
The Path to Passing

When I was doing my research into trans-related issues, I found a lot of discussion around the idea of "passing". Passing means being read as the gender you identify with. For me, identifying as a man meant being read that way. I studied articles and resources for young trans men about how best to pass as a man and started working hard on changing my behaviour. It was a difficult position, because I struggled with the idea that there were different behavioural standards for men and women, and I didn't agree with most of the things I was reading. But I was desperate to do anything to alleviate my gender dysphoria, and that meant conforming to behaviours I didn't necessarily identify with.

A phenomenon occurred for me during transition, whereby strangers on the street and in stores became more of a comfort than those closest to me. While my family and friends were adjusting to all these changes and dealing with them, I could walk into somewhere like a 7-Eleven and be read as a man. No dramas, no trouble and no emotional labour. I received more validation from people I didn't know than from those I had lived with my whole life. Of course this makes sense, but it was hard on an emotional level to face the people I love and feel silenced or drained around them. So I took the small comforts I received from strangers and held them closely.

Step 1: Clothing

The first step in passing as a man was buying more masculine clothing. I asked my mum if she would come with me, but she wanted nothing to do with it and told me she didn't know how to shop for boys. I went with Tia and friends. If you google "tips on passing" for transgender men, clothing is one of the first things that comes up. There are recommendations for styles that will take emphasis off hips, thighs and other parts that are considered "womanly". I changed my style and started wearing more button-up shirts and less tight-fitting clothing. I started hiding parts of my body and, essentially, hiding parts of myself in an effort to be seen as a man.

This was empowering, because I felt I had control over how I was read and I could be whoever I wanted to be. I felt powerful. In the long-term it didn't help me feel more connected to myself. I was pretending parts of me didn't exist. After putting it off for a long time, I went through my clothing and threw out all of the outfits I thought were too feminine. This is one of my biggest regrets. I spent so much time researching what it meant to be a man that I lost sight of what it meant to be me. But this was an important step in my journey of self-discovery. I needed to move on from who I was in order to discover who I could be. I got rid of everything. As I put one item of clothing after another into a bag, I cried. I saw it as a way of leaving my old self behind. And for the first time I felt I might miss her.

I wish I had known at the time that I could be a man in any shape or size, rather than changing myself to fit some narrow view of what it meant to be a man.

Step 2: Grooming

I already had short hair that could be tied into a topknot and the sides of my head were shaved. Then there was facial hair. I tried everything to encourage the hair-growth process before testosterone was an option. I read about how hair growth works and considered many different gimmicks. I started shampooing and conditioning my face because I had read it might help more hair grow. When I realised that didn't work, I researched ways I could create an illusion of facial hair. There were all sorts of complicated processes that involved cutting off bits of head hair and sticking them to your face using special theatre glue and make-up. It was all too much for me. Instead, I embraced the very light blond hairs I had around my face and started filling them in with mascara to simulate a stubble appearance. I hadn't interacted with mascara for so long and now suddenly needed to apply it every time I went out. Even though it didn't necessarily look anything like a beard, it definitely helped my confidence and eased my dysphoria, which was the more important thing for me.

I began being read as a man more and more. Each time it happened I felt validated and safe. I felt like people were seeing me for who I was. But it also highlighted the times I was read as a woman, and there was a very fine line that decided the direction the interaction would go. Many times someone would call me a man until they looked at me longer, or heard me speak, and then they would apologise and "correct" themselves. It felt like they were giving me a gift I desperately needed and then ripping it away. Every time I was misgendered my heart dropped. I felt heavier with the burden of correcting them, or accepting this assumption and holding it close to how I saw myself. While being gendered correctly was a victory, being seen as a woman was a failure to me, and proved I would never truly be who I believed myself to be.

Step 3: Packing

"Packing" refers to putting something in your pants to create a bulge. The whole idea is a little bit strange, because I really don't want people looking at my crotch – bulge or no bulge. If that's where someone looks to confirm my "manhood", then I'm not sure I want much to do with them. But I know there is a confidence that packing brings. I tried to pack with socks. I don't know if you've ever put socks in your pants – it's not that comfortable.

As usual, I turned to the internet. I was inundated with packing options and enormous price tags. Eventually, I found a product that was designed as a packer, but was hollow and useable also as a device to allow me to stand and pee as well as one that could be used during sex. It was marketed as a three-in-one product. I couldn't believe it existed. It was exactly what I wanted. It was expensive, so I focused my attention on working harder to earn the money for this thing I felt could really help me.

Step 4: Mannerisms

There were endless tips online for how to learn mannerisms considered "typical" for men. I tried to change my behaviour. Some of these things involved practising how to lower my voice. One tip suggested singing along with the radio by trying to sing male parts or a lower version of the female parts. I also changed the way I sat. I stopped crossing my legs and instead spread them apart to take up more space.

Websites told me to build more muscle, to look at my nails by creating a fist and turning it towards me rather than stretching my hands out straight, to walk with a certain confidence and stride, stand with legs spread and hands by my side rather than on my hips (that was something that took longer to adjust to) and many other uncompromising depictions of what it is "men" do. I became hyperaware of my every action in public, scrutinising my mannerisms to ensure they were always that of a man.

Passing is not simple for everyone. I was incredibly lucky that once I started dressing, acting and behaving in a certain way, I was passing as male most of the time. Once this happened, I wasn't sure I could continue going to the women's toilets. Toilets are probably something that people who aren't trans, gender diverse or questioning never have to think about. I was getting stared at whenever I went into the women's toilets, but I knew I wasn't ready for the men's. I was terrified of being harassed, or beaten up, or worse. For a long time, I stopped peeing in public toilets. I would time my toilet trips to ensure I wouldn't need to go once I was out of the house. I held my bladder on long days and tried my best to wait until I was home and safe. This became increasingly unrealistic. Where possible, I would go into the accessible toilets, but felt uneasy using them as an able-bodied person. I felt I was occupying a space I wasn't entitled to. On the very rare occasions I would find a gender-neutral bathroom, I almost cried.

I was becoming more confident in how often I was passing and took the opportunity to go to the men's toilets in an empty building when no one else was in there. I rushed in to the "men's", heart racing, and quickly locked the cubicle door. I had done it. I sat down, allowed myself to breathe and then peed. I was both terrified and relieved and acutely aware of the smell of urine that seemed absent in most women's toilets.

* * *

There was a lot on the net about etiquette in male bathrooms: details of which urinal to go to if someone is already peeing; how long one should spend looking in the mirror; and the general atmosphere of the men's room. I certainly wasn't used to people farting or burping loudly. I was very nervous about my first trip into a bathroom that actually had men in it. I learned to pee quickly so that I could make these journeys as painless as possible. I would run in, go to a cubicle, pee, quickly wash my hands, barely look at myself in the mirror in case I brought attention to myself and run out. It's funny how much more comfortable

I actually felt in the women's toilet. I wasn't anywhere near as afraid of women as I was of men. I remember when I first began using the men's room and my mum asked me whether it made me feel out of place seeing all of those penises. I had to explain that peeing was more of a priority than staring at strangers' junk.

Once I was a full-time male toilets user, another issue announced itself obnoxiously – menstruating in the men's room. There are no sanitary bins for your pads and tampons in the men's room. I was afraid to flush my tampons down the toilet because I had been told my whole life not to, and my anxious brain created scenarios where I did, clogged the toilet, flooded the place and then everyone saw my tampon. I looked up tips and tricks and settled on wrapping up my sanitary items in lots of toilet paper and subtly walking out of the cubicle and throwing them in the bin. I had never been this embarrassed about my period before. I was highly aware of the extra attention I could potentially be bringing to myself. The men's toilets never felt safe for me.

* * *

The whole journey of passing was incredibly important, but I hope that in future we can shift focus away from trans people needing to "pass". I don't need to sit, stand, walk and talk a certain way to be believed as a man. The only thing that should influence whether someone sees me as a man or not is how I identify. If that is what I say I am, it's as simple as that. I shouldn't need to meet rigid ideas of masculinity.

I'm not sure why moulding everyone into the same kind of person is so appealing anyway. There are many different ways to perform gender, and we should be open and encouraging of them. Passing served its purpose for me, and was crucial at the time, but it also resulted in a loss of identity. I wasn't sure any more how much of my behaviour was truly my authentic self and what was created as a means of being seen a certain way. In order to be seen and treated in the way I felt was appropriate, I had to meet many standards set by social norms. But I often found myself wondering, what does it actually mean to be a man? Or a woman? Who gets to decide these criteria? And why are we afraid to embrace notions of "other"?

* * *

Even though passing did a lot for my confidence, there were still moments when dysphoria took over. Tia and I went to a Tegan and Sara concert one night, which was the first time I had been surrounded by lesbians since coming out as a trans man. Tegan and Sara were an important part of being a lesbian for me. I discovered them on Tumblr when I was sixteen and began a lifelong love affair. They're Canadian twins who both identify as lesbians, and as a young girl-lover I identified strongly with their music. To hear songs that actually reflected the relationships I was in was affirming.

It should have been an incredible night. However, I felt anxious and paranoid that I would be read as a lesbian. I wish this hadn't bothered me. I had for so long identified as a lesbian and held that label close to me, but suddenly it had become distressing. I spent the night trying to convince myself that knowing I was a man was enough; I didn't have to be seen constantly as one to make it true. I ran my fingers along my very minimal facial hair. At that point I had started shaving my face to encourage growth – even though this is a myth – and the feeling of harsh stubble growing back comforted me. This, and feeling my chest with the binder on, became ways of minimising anxiety and tools to deal with my dysphoria. It was this night that made me realise being a trans man might mean I'm no longer a lesbian and that scared me.

I loved being a lesbian. It was always hard to find a place as a lesbian in the gay community because it was overrun with men. Every time I went to a gay party or club, it was filled with gay men. I'm glad that they have a safe place to express themselves, but I always wondered where mine was. I had spent a long time trying to find my own safe lesbian community and to a certain extent I had managed to do that. But the more male I looked, the less I felt welcome in this community. I suddenly wasn't sure where I fit in. I knew I wasn't a straight man. I wasn't a gay man either, and I didn't feel like I could be a lesbian any more. I felt a great loss of community. Especially because a lot of trans men I knew merely assimilated into groups of men, something I didn't really feel comfortable with. I didn't want to lose the queer community. I was part of a few online groups with trans men but I felt different from them and I wasn't sure why.

* * *

Nevo and Tia at their Year Twelve formal (2013)

There was always a complicated dynamic between my siblings and me, and I was terrified to talk to them about my gender. They had been accepting of my sexuality, but it was clear that we come from, and move in, different worlds. My siblings are amazing – they are accomplished, inspiring and beautiful people. I understand now that their reactions did not reflect how much they loved or cared about me. I know they have come to understand things more clearly and I know they did not mean to hurt me. But none of that changes the pain I felt at the time.

This is hard for me to write. I remember this stage of my life clearly, and all I want to do is forget it.

After I told my dad I was trans, I didn't feel ready to tell the rest of the family. I explicitly asked him not to tell my siblings as he had with my sexuality. I was exhausted by the depression and anxiety taking over my life. It was a constant battle and I didn't want to deal with everyone else and their reactions. It's difficult to comfort people about something you feel *you* need comforting over. I didn't have the emotional capacity at that point to support them through this change. I needed to support myself, and I wasn't doing it very well.

One evening I was at my dad's house and I was wearing my binder. My brother noticed my chest was flatter and asked me about it. I didn't want to go into it, but wasn't sure how else to explain it. He seemed genuinely worried about me, so I told him the truth.

Not long after, he invited me to come to his work after school one day to properly talk about my transition. I was anxious to the point of hyperventilating. I mustered up my educational energy and was prepared to answer any and all of the questions he had. I sat down in his office, where his wife was sitting with him. It seemed more that he wanted to speak *at* me, rather than hear what I had to say. It felt like a job interview, a "prove that you're really trans" interview. He asked me a lot of questions I couldn't possibly answer. "How do you know this won't change?" and "What exactly makes you feel like a man?" and "Why can't you just be happy being a lesbian?" I didn't have answers to these questions, only feelings. I acted with a certainty I didn't have, contradicted myself because I wasn't sure how to adequately respond, and this was used as evidence against me.

He told me my problem was I was insecure and had low self-esteem; that I should go and see a psychologist and fix the way I view myself. I knew this wasn't the problem. I had plenty of self-confidence most of the time and a relatively high self-esteem. I was going through a depressive period, but who didn't have times like that? Who didn't feel low sometimes? That wasn't reason enough to reject the feelings I was having towards my gender. He said if I transitioned I would always look like a freak and would never be believably male. I explained I was passing as a man about seventy per cent of the time. He told me I was delusional. He and his wife spoke about my age and lack of worldly understanding, that in time I would grow to discover new things about myself and shouldn't make life-altering choices right now. That would have been an important point – if this wasn't a matter of survival.

In regards to gender issues, there is only a certain extent to which you can intellectualise things, the rest is pure emotion. I knew what I needed to feel authentically myself, to continue my life and be the best person I could be. I couldn't necessarily explain it succinctly, but I shouldn't have had to. I knew what I needed for me. I left his office deflated and more depressed than when I had entered. I had spent so much time convincing myself not to be trans, I certainly didn't need it coming from anyone else.

My other brother also couldn't understand why I would want or need to transition. First, he tried to empower me and commend me for being a strong lesbian woman of whom he was proud, but what I heard was that he wouldn't be proud of me if I were anything else. I felt his love and support was conditional on the image I had been performing. He then claimed I wouldn't be a real man without a penis and it wouldn't be worth being in an in-between zone that would confuse people. We went back and forth with emails, sending each other articles about gender issues. I sent him plenty that I would now disagree with, but at the time I didn't understand transgender politics. I was desperately looking for anything that could make sense of the feelings I was having. He tried to use trans statistics of suicide and depression as evidence of transition regret among trans people, not understanding that those statistics were the result of discrimination and not remorse about their own gender transition. He didn't realise that by aggressively challenging my gender identity he was contributing to these statistics, rather than minimising them.

My sister didn't ask difficult and intimately personal questions, she took more of a medical perspective. As a medical professional, she was concerned with the effects I might experience through transition. She understood I was trans and didn't question it, but she wanted to ensure I was making informed decisions about my process. These were incredibly validating questions because I had done plenty of research and I could actually answer them. I could tell she appreciated that and saw how seriously I was taking the idea of medical intervention. I felt safe with her and turned to her often when I needed family support. I was grateful to have her and it made us closer. I think she also helped other members of my family come to understand and support me.

My siblings got better in time. A lot of the initial reactions were emotionally driven and once they had more time to process and come to terms with things, issues were resolved. But the damage had been done, and I didn't feel understood by them. My coming-out experiences with my brothers created a large rift between us. I was hurt by their reactions and, at a time when I already hated myself, the defensiveness and aggression I received made everything worse.

I made each of my immediate family members a booklet called "How to be a supportive family member". I compiled articles I felt were relevant and hoped this would result in more understanding. After a long while my siblings started calling me their brother and using my new name and pronouns. I mostly felt tolerated, rather than embraced and cared for. I felt very othered in my family, and that I always had to justify myself around them. I was told that I spoke of my gender or queer issues too much and should try to expand my conversation topics.

Nevo's Year Twelve school photo (2013)

CHAPTER 8
SCHOOL IS A BATTLEFIELD

I had a big dilemma about coming out at school, as if it wasn't a minefield enough without being transgender. I had only about six months until I was finished with school forever, and I wasn't sure it was worth having to go through the whole social transition process. The dynamics at my very small private Jewish school were quite entrenched; I wasn't sure how this coming out would go. I had many internal debates between my political self and my personal self. The political side asserted that this was important, as it would expose people to gender issues and would be a unique educational opportunity. It would help gender diverse people to come through the school in the future or even the Jewish community at large. But my personal self was terrified. I wasn't sure I had the energy to educate because I was too mentally fragile. I put the thought away and tried to continue going to school as before. I didn't want to bring attention to any changes so I continued to wear the girl's uniform, which meant a dress in summer and a skirt in winter.

I struggled to focus at school. I thought I could ignore my gender issues for a few more months but it started affecting my relationships. I felt like I was lying to everyone, and more importantly, that I was lying to myself. It was distressing for me to wear a dress every day and all I could think about was whether the people around me would accept who I truly was, and not the self I was choosing to show. My internal dialogue was deafening. I couldn't escape myself. These thoughts dominated and I wasn't able to participate in conversations. I had terrible nightmares that I would come to school in a dress and people would taunt me.

I started wearing pants to school and the teachers got on my back about it. I didn't want to sit everyone down and make an announcement, but I also didn't want to have the same conversation over and over. I needed to find my truth.

We had a Facebook group with everyone in Year Twelve and after a lot of consideration I sent the following message:

"Hey guys, I'd like to make this as brief as I possibly can but apologise in advance if I don't succeed. Before I explain what this is about, I'd like to initially entrench in all of your minds

how open I am about this and that I will absolutely welcome any questions any of you have. I'd also really appreciate if this wasn't discussed behind my back but rather with me as I'm not ashamed, nor embarrassed and would like to enlighten all of those who do not understand. I'd preferably like this information to stay within the school but if there are people you'd like to tell then please just ask me first.

Basically, recently I've had a lot of self-reflection and have discovered that I am transgender. For those of you who do not know what this means, in short, it means that my mind and body do not match up in the sense that, in my mind I feel like I am male but my body is that of a female. Now that's not a great definition and obviously it'll bring a lot of confusion. I never really understood it myself either. So please research it or ask me questions if you're unsure of what this means.

Starting from next term, I'd like to be referred to with male pronouns (he, him) and my preferred male name which is Nevo (pronounced Neh-voh) but everyone can just call me Nev. I've already spoken to most of my teachers about it and everyone has been extremely understanding and supportive. Now I recognise that this is a huge change and will take a long time for everyone to adjust to. So please don't stress if you stuff up or make any mistakes, I'm really fine with it, I just truly appreciate people trying and as long as you're comfortable with it, I'll be happy to correct you as it's something I already do internally now anyway.

I wanted to bring this up now rather than during the holidays so that you guys have the opportunity to speak to me in person about this if you choose to and also have a little more time to adjust to the thought. I appreciate all the support I have already received and really hope all of you can engage with that."

The response to my coming out to the year level was quite surprising – there wasn't one. A few people commented and commended me on my bravery. Others messaged me privately to show their support, but in general I didn't hear from the majority of people. I assumed it was a non-issue and felt relieved. I expected things would change at school, that people would treat me differently or approach me with unending questions. However nothing changed, everything was exactly the same, no one had any questions for me. I didn't understand but I preferred no reaction to a bad one. The first instance it was brought up publicly was when I walked into a literature classroom and everyone had shifted seats. I liked to sit in the same seat every day, and so I felt displaced and confused. I asked what was going on and said I hated change, to which another student responded, "Really? Coming from you?" which I thought was quite funny.

Soon it became clear my coming out hadn't been as well received as I thought. People had been talking about me behind my back, claiming that I was attention-seeking and rejecting that I could ever transition to be a man. I felt insecure and lonely at school for the rest of the year. The teachers were quite good and tried hard. They were afraid of making mistakes with my pronouns but at that point I had plenty of patience to help walk them through it. It got to a stage where they began correcting themselves if they made mistakes, or other students would, and I was able to relax a bit.

The main issue for me with coming out at school was that I was still very new to the ideas of gender transition and gender politics. I was only beginning to learn these things myself, and yet I was expected to teach everyone else. I sent articles to teachers and had meetings with them, trying to work out where the appropriate place to go to the bathroom would be, what uniform I could wear and so forth. It was a tiring process, one I couldn't help wish had already been established through policy. I like to think that in future, the journey will be easier for gender diverse students in that school because the administration have a better understanding now.

We decided it would be more appropriate for me to use the accessible toilet rather than the men's, because I hadn't come out to everyone in the school and I didn't feel safe going in there. It was very different going into men's toilets in public with people that didn't know me, compared to the toilets at school. I went to the accessible toilet even though

I didn't feel entitled to that space either, but was grateful to be offered a safe place to pee. Luckily, I was in Year Twelve and didn't have to deal with gender-divided school sports. I tried to change the name on my school email but my principal was concerned I might change my mind and it wouldn't be reversible. The "irreversible" concern has come up many times throughout my transition.

Life at school continued as usual and I tried to get through the last few months without completely breaking down. I kept to my studies and myself and mostly only interacted with my friends. I avoided the people I knew were talking about me behind my back. The thing that got me through was knowing that regardless of what I did or what happened, high school would inevitably end, and I wouldn't have to see anyone I didn't want to see ever again.

* * *

In preparation for the advertising degree I was considering undertaking, I went to a creative workshop at RMIT in the mid-year school holidays. By this point I was passing as a man most of the time in one-off interactions. Usually as soon as I opened my mouth to speak, people would hear my voice, they would correct themselves and apologise. This was the first full day I went being read as a man.

At one point we were doing an activity where we had

to brainstorm ideas for a mascara product. The tutor asked us what we thought were the reasons why women wear mascara between the ages of fifteen and thirty-five. A debate began and a girl stood up and explained that those are the primary ages when women are vying for the attention of men, and that usually by age thirty-five, women have settled down with a husband and are no longer on "the hunt". I had been anxious the whole day because I was worried someone would misgender me or question the fact that I was a man, so I was terrified to rebut what I considered a grossly inaccurate statement. Yet I stood up and tried to explain that women do not necessarily buy make-up and use it for the attention of men; that this does not take into account women of different sexual orientations, or those who use make-up as an art form of self-expression. Also, it is highly unlikely if a woman has been wearing mascara her entire life that she would stop because she was married. I went on to talk a bit more about beauty standards in the media and the misogyny intrinsically connected to it.

The applause I received afterwards was embarrassing. As a woman feminist I was laughed at, ridiculed and not taken seriously. But in a room filled with people who read me as a man, seeing a man stick up for women's rights and women's issues was commended. I had never before been positively regarded for being a feminist and I was acutely aware the only thing that had changed was people's reading of my gender. This proved to me that people respect men more than women, even in issues concerning women.

Being read as a man in feminist spaces brought new problems. I felt strange speaking on behalf of women's issues, as someone who was assumed to be a man. I held the oppressions of my past closely and in situations where I was read as a cisgender man, I wasn't sure how to express that without being seen as a mansplainer.

* * *

Any anxieties I had about school came to a climax with plans for muck-up day. Muck-up day was an opportunity for Year Twelves to have a little fun, mess up the school a bit and have an assembly celebrating the year level. The assembly consisted of three dances: a group dance with everyone, a boys' dance and a girls' dance. Rehearsals began and I realised I hadn't been invited to either the girls' or the boys' dances. I figured it was an oversight and told one of the guys. He explained that the boys were refusing to have me in their dance. My heart dropped. I hadn't even considered that this would be an issue or the decision would be made behind my back, without any input from me.

I asked for more information from others and found out there had been recent debate in the boys' WhatsApp group (which I didn't know existed) about my gender identity and its validity. I was devastated. I couldn't look at any of the boys. I wasn't sure who was on which side of the debate and who was discussing intimate details about my body.

I didn't go to school for a few days; I couldn't. This incident brought back a lot of difficult memories of the bullying I experienced as a child and I began to panic. I desperately wanted to run away from everything – from school, from the boys, from myself. I reached out to my friends, all of whom were girls, and they informed me they didn't want to get involved in the discussion. They weren't particularly confrontational and I think they were afraid of the boys. I went back to school and tried to put on a brave face.

While I was absent, a small group of boys had gone to the admin office, demanding action against the bullying I was a victim of. I don't think the school administration knew how to handle this dilemma. The response was, "Perhaps if this is causing trouble, she should not be part of the dance." Wrong pronoun, misgendered. And they obviously hadn't got the memo that victim-blaming is not the best way to address bullying issues.

The boys were unsatisfied with this response and made a Facebook group with other allies in the year level and tried to brainstorm the best way to fix the situation. I didn't know any of this was going on and was appreciative when

I found out, but I also felt vulnerable that a discussion relating to me was happening without my voice. I felt powerless, and at the same time was upset to the point I wasn't sure I had the capacity to be involved. Eventually, the principal called a meeting for the year level. She sat everyone down and explained that being transgender is a valid identity. To hear that affirmation come from a religious Jewish woman was amazing. From this followed a debate between my side of the room defending me and the other side arguing against.

I felt dehumanised to have people talking about my gender identity as if I wasn't present. People kept looking at me throughout and I had to pretend their piercing stares and hateful words weren't hurting me deeply. The outcome was that I was allowed to be part of the dance. I respectfully declined the invitation. The conversation was more important than the result anyway. On muck-up day, I sat back as the boys and girls did their dances and hid the tears I felt welling up.

* * *

I was ready to change my name on Facebook, then I realised there were people who may not be as ready for the change as I was. There were family members, family friends and others that I hadn't yet come out to. I didn't feel it appropriate to do it through a Facebook name change, so I deleted them. I started with the people most emotionally removed from me and then went closer with family friends and family. Maybe this wouldn't seem as significant to people from a different generation, or those who have managed to escape the tight grips of Facebook addiction, but deleting people close to me was a devastating experience.

Facebook is an important part of my life. It's a way to stay in touch with people – especially people I don't often catch up with, or those who live far away. It is also a network for me to reach out to other trans people around the world and receive support that I don't have access to in person.

I got rid of a lot of people. I wasn't hiding from them or shutting them out, I was trying to protect them. The one that upset me the most was deleting my mum. I kept imagining the moment when I would add each of them back. Would they accept me, and how much of that acceptance would be limited to the online world?

* * *

The situation with my mum wasn't improving. I had thought she was dealing with things in her own time, but she wasn't confronting my transition at all, rather she was pushing it to the side and hoping it would go away. I was faced with a difficult dilemma. I had to decide whether to give my mum more time and space to process the news, or whether to give her a bit more of a push. I wanted to be patient and understanding with her, but it was coming at the cost of my own mental health. I dreaded going home every day and didn't feel I could be myself. I wanted her to understand the seriousness of the situation.

I had a few more conversations with her, then realised she needed to speak to people who were more detached from the situation. At separate points I got Shannon and Tia to sit with her and talk everything through. I think it helped. It was easier for her to grasp the situation when she was able to talk it out with other people without my presence. They tried to help her see how she could better support me, and shifted emphasis on how my transition was affecting her back onto how it was affecting me. It was through these conversations that something clicked for my mum.

Once it happened, it seemed an almost overnight change. Mum bought some books about supporting trans children and started reading those and other materials that I had sent to her. She was finally ready to listen and let me in. Slowly, she began calling me her son and used my new name. Our relationship became much closer; in fact, she became my biggest advocate.

I am incredibly grateful to my mother. We do a lot

of activist work together in the community, which is wonderful. I am impressed at how she was able to overcome her difficulties and accept and love me for who I am. Although I still feel pain in regards to how she treated me at the beginning of my transition, her ability to take responsibility for her mistakes and apologise is what has saved our relationship.

* * *

After I came out to my year level, a girl in my class messaged me and said she knew someone indirectly who was also trans, and if I needed support I should try to reach out to him. At that point I had never actually spoken to another trans man. I found this guy on Facebook and sent him a message. We began speaking and I asked him a lot of questions. He was extremely patient and helped me see things from a different perspective. He encouraged the idea that I could have a future, and be happy with myself, and that the dysphoria I'd been experiencing would pass, or at least I would learn how to deal with it better. He also debunked some myths surrounding testosterone. He explained it's not a wonder drug that would solve everything and I should be seeking help for any mental and emotional stuff I was going through. He told me the changes would be very gradual and dependent on my genetics, and described the process he went through in Melbourne to get testosterone and surgery. This advice was very different to what was online, which was mostly from men in America. It was the first time I had spoken face to face with someone who understood. I felt hopeful and positive.

Something that struck me was that he couldn't remember how long it had been since he had chest surgery. I was blown away by the fact that his life didn't revolve around his transition. He wasn't counting the months or years since gender-related milestones and they were not the only things dictating his life. I longed for this to be my life too. The most significant thing he told me was I was going to need to stop trying to be a man. I was shocked; he sounded exactly like my family and friends. I thought he understood me, but this comment hurt. He went on to explain, *"I don't mean that you're not a man, but you're not a cis-man. You are never going to be a cis-man. You'll probably never have a functioning penis, and you won't be like other men in that way. That's okay, because you're your own type of man, exactly as you are. You don't have to change anything or try to be like other guys. You can just be you, you're a trans-man, and that's a special kind of man because you're not like everyone else, you're you."*

In that moment, I was offended and disheartened. I wanted to believe I could eventually be like any other man; I could have a penis and assimilate into the regulated gender norms ascribed to men. I didn't want to think of myself as different. Over time however, I began to see that maybe the things I had been reading about being a man weren't true. I could do whatever I wanted. It did not matter how people read me, whether it was as a woman or a man, because regardless, I was being true to myself and that's what mattered the most. This was crucial advice and needed to come from another trans person who intimately understood. It took a long while to allow myself to address those statements, but they have since stuck with me throughout my transition.

Nevo and their mum, Sharon, at their high school graduation (2013)

Chapter 9
Testing Testosterone

The process to get on testosterone was going to be long and arduous and I felt the need to begin as soon as possible. As usual, I had done my research and knew that the best place for me to go would be the Monash Gender Dysphoria Clinic. I had to send in a letter, with a referral from a GP and a psychologist. I got the documents together and sent them in as quickly as I could. I was excited to see a doctor or medical professional who specialised in gender. When I didn't hear from them for a while, I called to see what was happening. It turned out that there was a very long waiting list to even get an appointment, let alone to get approval for testosterone. I was unable to get testosterone until I was eighteen without going to family court. I was about seven months away from turning eighteen.

Eventually, I had to make the call to bypass the waiting

lists and go to see the gender psychiatrist, which meant more out-of-pocket expenses. Being able to do this was an immense privilege. My parents could see how much I was struggling and were willing to assist financially with the appointments, and this coupled with the Medicare rebates we received meant I was able to book my first appointment with Dr Fintan Harte in July 2013.

I took the tram from school. I was nervous and terribly eager for the appointment. Fintan greeted me and welcomed me into his rooms. Mostly we spoke about my childhood, times I felt I was a boy, how my family had interacted with me throughout my life and through my coming outs. He did tests and examinations and asked me strange questions I didn't understand the relevance of. It took five months, six sessions and a significant amount of money, but he eventually gave me the referral to the endocrinologist who would be responsible for writing my testosterone script. The whole medical process was gruelling and I think if I went through it now, it wouldn't be as simple. At the time, I felt I had been born in the wrong body, that I was a man trapped in a woman's body. This is the kind of language the medical world loves. It is textbook for transgender people, and therefore I was more likely to get the medical treatment I needed if I felt this way. This is no longer how I feel, and therefore I think I would have struggled far more now to attain the same treatment. I needed to be a certain kind of transgender person to be taken seriously and given the support that I needed.

While both my parents were struggling with my transition, I suggested that after my gender assessment they should speak to Fintan directly and get a medical perspective. They were both apprehensive about me taking testosterone and I thought this could be helpful. They needed to see him individually, as they weren't exactly on speaking terms, so I organised an appointment for each of them. My mum had come to understand things better and had read books and resources on supporting her trans child. She asked Fintan questions and he seemed impressed with the level of love and support she was willing to offer. He assured her testosterone would likely be the right pathway for me and spoke of the many clients he had worked with over the years who had gone on to live healthy and fulfilling lives after undergoing medical transition.

Dad had a hard time wrapping his head around the idea of me taking testosterone. He was confused about the situation and throughout the appointment he used the wrong pronouns and messed up my name. By the end the doctor pointed this out, and suggested he needed to take time to think about my transition and try to adjust. My dad said he needed a one hundred per cent guarantee testosterone would be the right thing for me. The doctor responded that this was not possible. There was no scientific test that had been done specifically on me to produce that kind of result. However, he could tell my dad through experience, research, knowledge and understanding that there was about a ninety-seven per cent chance taking testosterone would enhance the quality of my life. Dad said afterwards that he felt attacked during the appointment, as if Fintan and I had ganged up on him and he didn't have the time or space to process everything.

* * *

Despite everything I had gone through in my last few months of high school, I managed to do well in my exams. I worked hard and enjoyed the academic side of my schooling. I didn't enjoy the pressure placed on me or on the numbered rank that I would produce, that would apparently determine my worth. I got a great result, but it meant very little to me. I couldn't wait to leave school forever and discover what my life could be like outside of that constricting institution. I threw out the huge piles of notes I had made and the bandaids I used to cover my piercings, and I cut up my uniform.

I was excited to think I would now be able to express myself however I wanted. I would not be told how to dress or present myself. I was free.

I had a ten-month trip to Israel and travel afterwards

to look forward to. I needed to work hard to raise enough money to go away. I got two jobs as well as other odd tasks and worked about ten-hour days on average from as soon as I finished school until I went away. I needed money for my doctor's appointments and testosterone, which was going to cost me about $100 a month. While working, I made a very difficult decision to create a crowdfunding website to help fundraise for my testosterone. I felt strange about it because in so many ways I was privileged and capable of working and earning my own money. I spoke to many people about it and received the support I needed. I wasn't forcing anyone to donate; it was there as an extra helping hand, and it did help. I worked in a charity call centre and an electronic toyshop. These were the first jobs I had ever worked where people read me as a man and didn't know I was trans. I had been out as trans at a job in the past, but because I had transitioned while there, my boss frequently made mistakes and this influenced how customers treated me. They would initially gender me as male, and as soon as pronoun mistakes were made, they would quickly shift their perceptions.

It was easier for me starting new jobs, where people knew me only by the name by which I introduced myself. But I wasn't sure what to do when signing work contracts, which required my name, title and gender. I didn't want to out myself as trans at work, but was concerned about the legalities of being truthful on my forms. I decided that for my safety it was better to tick the male box and write "Mr".

I was misgendered over the phone many times at the call centre, which highlighted the anxiety I already had over my voice. Once I was speaking to a man over the phone, trying to get him to donate to a charity I was representing. He said, "Darling, did you know it's my birthday? Would you give me a kiss? I'm sixty today, sweetheart." I had to explain I was a man and he immediately became apologetic. He only wanted to flirt inappropriately if I was a woman.

Another day, one of my co-workers at the call centre pulled a friend of mine aside and asked her if I was actually a boy, because I had such a "pretty" face. I overheard the conversation and felt my stomach stir with anxiety. She mocked me when she thought I wasn't looking, and when I confronted my boss, he told me to ignore her. I enjoyed working at the toyshop much more because flying helicopters are more exciting than phone conversations, but also I was being read as male the entire time. Read as a fourteen-year-old boy rather than my actual age, but a boy nonetheless.

As I became closer with my co-workers at the toyshop, a new issue arose. I realised there were parts of my past I couldn't discuss without revealing I was trans. It became difficult to navigate telling stories and I had to change them in order to reflect having lived as a man my whole life.

Although this felt disingenuous, I was excited to be treated as a man and I didn't care about erasing certain parts of my past. However, being treated as a man meant really being treated as *a man*. Other male co-workers assumed they were in good company and would say misogynistic things to me as women passed the shop. I wanted to call them out over this behaviour, yet at the same time I was terrified that doing so would out me as trans, and I would lose the belonging I felt. I never managed to stay silent over these comments because they made me angry, but I also didn't stand up as much as I could have.

* * *

Before going to see the endocrinologist and talking about the potential of beginning testosterone, I wanted to find out the effects it would have on my reproductive system and whether I would still be able to have children. I wanted to explore the option of freezing my eggs so I could have biological children. Though I knew that if this was not possible, I would adopt children or find another way to have them.

I had received varying advice from different medical professionals, so I decided to go to an IVF specialist. I spent $300 to find out this woman was not the right person to talk to. Because I hadn't made a concrete decision, there wasn't much she could help me with aside from informing me that freezing my eggs for approximately ten years would cost me about $7000. She also explained it was likely testosterone would ruin my reproductive system and it wouldn't be an option to have children once I began taking it, and I should consider that before deciding not to freeze.

I started thinking about why biological children were actually important to me and how I would feel if that wasn't possible. A lot of my hang-ups regarding the need to have children biologically related to me were definitely influenced and indoctrinated by societal standards. I knew I would always find a way to have a child. If it was meant to be, things would work themselves out in regards to testosterone. I knew I needed to be on testosterone to feel secure in myself and validated. I desperately wanted the effects it would bring, and I understood that it could mean a sacrifice I may later regret. But at that point there was no other choice outside of testosterone. So I tried to detach myself from the idea of biological children.

I went to see the endocrinologist with my mum on the same day I had seen the IVF specialist. He was a polite older man, very relaxed, and did not reciprocate the excitement I was feeling over the possibility that I could receive my testosterone script. He explained the possible side effects – the good ones, the bad ones and the fairly scary ones. Mum sat there and nodded and he told her she was taking this surprisingly well. She responded, "Well, what choice do I have?" And he said, "You wouldn't believe how many people I get in here who come without their family's support. Who have been kicked out of their homes and are on their own." To which she replied, "It hasn't been easy, but this is my child. I have to be here to support and love them regardless. They are the same person, just a different package." And I knew Mum had finally begun to understand. I needed her during this, and it felt like she was finally there. I let out a breath I felt I had been holding for months.

The endocrinologist explained that it was possible to come off the medication for a certain period and that my ovulation cycle and periods would resume as normal. But testosterone affects different people in various ways and there isn't very much research into these matters. Of course it wasn't very comforting to receive totally contradictory advice from different medical professionals, but it's something that, as a trans person, I have adjusted to. The most important thing was to be on testosterone; it was the only thing getting me out of bed every morning. That was more important than protecting my unborn children that didn't yet exist. I needed to protect myself.

The doctor handed me the testosterone prescription and my knuckles turned white from holding it so tight.

I couldn't believe I had it in my hands. The future looked brighter. The future looked existent.

* * *

Aside from the medical difficulties and waiting lists and fees I had to face to get my testosterone script, there was a lot more that went into the decision. I felt that every force was working against me starting testosterone, and that was difficult because I had been struggling for a long time and was counting on it. I thought people would understand how important it was to me and that I wasn't making this decision lightly. Even though I was aware it wasn't an all-in-one solution to my mental health issues, I knew gender affirmation in any form would allow me to live a better life.

My own brain working overtime had consumed me and it became difficult to think of others and be a better person. I was self-involved and anxious. I wanted silence so I could refocus my life with others at the centre, rather than just myself. I wanted to be less mentally exhausted. Many people around me didn't understand.

I was only a few months away from eighteen. Shortly after my birthday, I would be travelling to Israel with Habo to engage in a year-long leadership program. I wanted to start testosterone right away but there were a few things holding me back.

Tia was afraid. We had been together for three years. There was uncertainty surrounding the future of our relationship, and the gender stuff mixed in there complicated things further. Although Tia had been exceptionally understanding and supportive throughout my transition, when it came to testosterone I think it enhanced an insecurity that she had already. She thought I would change too much while away and we would not be able to rebuild a relationship when I returned. She wanted to be a part of my transition and didn't like the idea of me potentially coming home a different person.

My family was against the idea of me going on testosterone while I was away. I think they were nervous about the trip in general. It would be the longest time I'd been away from them, and that coupled with the potential of me physically transitioning was too much. They were concerned that I would change while overseas and they would no longer recognise me. They were worried about how young I was and felt I wasn't self-aware enough to be certain that this was the right thing. They also wanted me to go through the journey with my family to support me and were worried I wouldn't have enough support from the people I was travelling with.

But I didn't feel particularly supported by my family. Although they were slowly coming to terms with my transition, I still felt deeply hurt by how some of them had invalidated and patronised me. I didn't necessarily feel safe around them, so it didn't make sense that I should wait to be with them.

My dad didn't understand the rush to take testosterone and my mum and I had many long arguments about it. The funny thing was we were both arguing the same point – we didn't want my transition to be at the forefront of my year. We both wanted me to focus on the program I was on, the relationships I would be building and the volunteer work I would be doing. But we had radically different ideas of how that could be attained.

I argued that I needed the hormones in order for my gender to be affirmed. I was nervous about being in a different country as an only-sometimes-passing trans boy – especially Israel, where social cues are different and people tend to be less filtered than Australians. Hebrew is a gendered language and I was worried I would be misgendered constantly, which would have a very significant effect on my mental health. At least if I was taking testosterone, I would feel like I was making progress. Mum thought if I was on testosterone it would isolate me from the rest of my group and shift my focus primarily onto my transition. She didn't understand I needed to be on it in order to stop thinking about it.

All I wanted was for my gender issues to be pushed to the back of my mind because I wanted to focus on bigger things.

* * *

Due to a very serious lack of understanding about testosterone and its effects, there were some concerns in my youth movement, Habo, surrounding me taking the medication while in their care and on their program. I went out for dinner one night with one of my leaders and she explained the coordinators of the program had decided that I must choose between testosterone and the year-long program. I broke down. She said she felt awful, telling me that the movement I had been a part of my whole life was not going to support me through this. I began pleading to the people higher up in the movement to find a way around this. I sent letters from my doctor, psychiatrist, endocrinologist, my psychologist and myself in an attempt to educate them about testosterone and its effects and how it would affect my year away. I thought their decision was grounded in ignorance and a misunderstanding of the process.

Their concern was that I would be living in close quarters with fifteen other people for the year. They were unsure how the testosterone would affect my mood and interactions and worried it could contribute negatively to an already intense social situation.

I agreed to wait until I returned from Israel before taking testosterone. But with each day, this decision lay heavy on my shoulders. This promise felt wrong and I wasn't sure how I would make it through another year feeling the way I was in my body. I viewed my dysphoria as a serious medical condition and couldn't understand why people would ask me to wait until things got worse before treating it. I needed to fix what was happening to me. Testosterone was urgent.

I spoke with my parents about the importance of testosterone for my mental health. They eventually agreed that I could start taking it slightly earlier. I was leaving for Israel at the end of January 2014 and the agreement was I could start in August 2014. Also, I would only be on a half dose for the first few months while my body became accustomed to the medication. This meant minimal change, but at least it would be something.

I had filled the testosterone script and had it to take to Israel because it would likely be hard to access while overseas. Having the medication in my room made things a lot more real. I began counting the months till I could take it. I was starting on testosterone gel rather than injections, because it'd be easier to transport overseas and to administer myself. It would involve rubbing the serum on my upper arms and stomach. When I looked at it, I saw the possibilities for my future. I could see facial hair, muscles, a low voice and what I most longed for: comfort and happiness. I wanted it desperately. I saw it as a solution to many of my problems. I sat counting each individual packet, ensuring it was all there.

Two weeks before going away, Habo conducted a seminar with the group of people I was going with to prepare us for the program. The seminar was geared towards logistics as well as building relationships with the people we would be living with. There were about thirty-two people from Perth, Sydney and Melbourne and we were divided into two groups. We had a few conversations about our expectations for the year, our concerns and the support we would need. I asked my friends how they felt about living with a transgender person and if they were apprehensive about potential side effects that could come from me taking testosterone. Everyone seemed understanding and unfazed. Mostly they were confused as to why I was waiting until August to start when I was clearly distressed. I offered the explanations and justifications I had rehearsed in my head from other people's words. But the more I said them, the less they made sense. My friends asked why I wasn't starting as soon as I turned eighteen and I could no longer think of any reasons that came exclusively from me. Other people's voices had taken over and I had lost my own. My voice was the most desperate, the most in need and the most affected. I needed to listen to my own voice.

I once did a first-aid course where they taught us that when someone is unconscious and not breathing they are in the worst situation they could possibly be in. Their airways are the total priority. While conducting CPR, you can accidentally break a few ribs, or injure another part of the person in order to save them, but it doesn't matter, because they couldn't possibly be worse off than they were at that point in time. The only important thing was to save them. This is how I felt about taking testosterone. I didn't care if I would maybe one day in the future regret it, or if the effects were not what I anticipated. I didn't care if it made me a "real" man, or if some relationships would be affected along the way. I know that sounds incredibly selfish, but that's because it was. I needed to go on testosterone for my survival, and I'm not sure I would be here today had I not. So I made the most difficult decision of my life. I went against the opinion and decisions of the people I loved and trusted the most, and I decided to take testosterone as soon as I got to Israel.

CHAPTER 10
I Am Not a Box

I revealed to everyone the decision I had made to bypass my August testosterone date and start as soon as I arrived in Israel. I was anxious and needed their support. My parents reacted badly. They felt I was going behind their backs after we had settled on a later time to take the medication. They didn't understand that the compromise had mostly been mine. Tia was angry too. I felt like everyone was against me.

There was also the issue of whether the coordinators of the program would allow me to take the testosterone. I had still not received an official answer from Habo. I decided to wait until I arrived in Israel. Whether I began then and there, or tried to plead with them further, depended on their answer.

I felt my year away was going to be transitional in many ways. I was embarking on a leadership program with passionate young activists determined to engage critically with Israel. I knew I was going to change. I was going to develop ideologically – living apart from my family would lead to significant growth. I would deal with intense and challenging social situations, and it made sense to add testosterone to the mix because shying away from one kind of transition while everything else was going to change didn't make any sense. It was a year of transition.

I was scared to go overseas, and the reality is I was scared to take testosterone. I had been dealing so much with other people's concerns that I didn't have any time to think about my own relationship with the medication. All I had been thinking about was the positives. There wasn't enough space for me to be scared because then I would feel like I was just succumbing to my family's worries. I wasn't sure how I would change. I was worried I would grow away from my friends and from Tia, and that petrified me. The idea of leaving for a year was scary. At the airport, walking away from my family, friends and Tia, I had never felt more alone. I turned my back to them as I entered the tunnel leading to the plane. I had no idea what was waiting for me and who I would be when I came home.

* * *

The day after my arrival in Israel I spoke to the program

coordinator and asked for her verdict on me taking testosterone. She said that no one would know whether I took it or not, she hadn't received a straight answer about it, and I should do what I thought was right for me. I appreciated this answer. I knew she couldn't explicitly tell me it was okay without approval from the head of the movement, but she also knew it was no one's business but mine. So on 29 January 2014, cramped in a small bathroom in a hotel in Tel Aviv with two friends, I applied my testosterone gel for the first time. I was away from judgement, disapproval and misunderstanding, and I felt free to do what I knew I had needed to do for a long time. I walked out of that bathroom the same person that had gone in. The world hadn't ended and everything was going to be okay. I was sure I'd done the right thing.

I wasn't going to experience any significant changes for a while, particularly on a half-dose, but there was something comforting in the thought that there was testosterone coursing through my veins. I felt peaceful, like I didn't need to fight my body any more. It was going to start doing what I wanted it to.

Meanwhile, I was attending a seminar with members of other Jewish youth movements as an opening to the program we were about to begin. The seminar was an interesting time. I was surrounded by a lot of people I didn't know and passing significantly less than I was used to. Many of my fellow attendees had never met someone who wasn't cisgender (that they knew of), and many were quite religious. I knew they would not understand or approve of my lifestyle and I definitely didn't feel safe coming out to them. I felt paranoid about how I was being read. I didn't have the chance to run off and talk to my friends about my feelings, so I internalised them.

I was scared of being outed as trans because I thought that would compromise the many gender-divided activities in the seminar, such as prayers, sleeping arrangements and bathrooms. I was worried I would be completely isolated if people knew, and that meant every time I was misgendered, I wasn't just concerned about being seen as who I truly was, I was worried about my safety. It didn't feel right hanging out with the guys; we were very different. And I was apprehensive about spending too much time with the girls, as it could be an indicator I wasn't like the other men. The seminar lasted a week and as soon as I was alone with the members of my own movement, I felt safer.

* * *

I was finding that testosterone allowed me to focus on other things. Gender was no longer at the forefront of my mind because I had a newfound comfort in my body. Knowing that changes were happening slowly felt like a daily affirmation and evidence I could be whoever I wanted to be. And because changes were gradual, I wasn't as obsessed with monitoring them as I had anticipated. I thought I would scrutinise every minor change, make videos and comparison photos, but I was so busy and distracted that I wasn't overly conscious of how I looked, which I think was very positive. Had I transitioned while at home, I believe I would have paid far more attention to the little details. I'm glad that, for the most part, my mind was elsewhere. I began a transition channel on YouTube like many trans people before me had done. I wanted to offer something in return after those channels had done so much for me. I made a video every month.

Changes were happening. I was grateful my period stopped earlier than expected. It wasn't necessarily something that caused me stress, but it was certainly a major inconvenience I was happy to be rid of. Plus I would save plenty of money on sanitary items.

My voice began to drop, hair grew in places it hadn't before like my stomach, toes and upper arms, veins began to pop out more, my appetite increased dramatically and I gained a lot of weight. This was scary because of my turbulent history with weight and exercise, but I was in such a safe environment that I was surprised to find it didn't bother me. Plus being exposed to new and exciting oily Middle Eastern food meant a lot of people were gaining weight alongside me. Over time I developed more acne, more pronounced muscles, a change in body odour, my face became fuller, my voice cracked more frequently and I had significant struggles with crying. It wasn't that I didn't want to cry; I absolutely love crying. I think testosterone halted my tear production and made it a lot more difficult to cry. *That* made me want to cry. My voice changed and it hurt my throat to sing too high. I became self-conscious about my voice and the loss of range I was experiencing, and I stopped singing completely for over a year.

With each day on testosterone my dysphoria was alleviating, however I still felt different to the people I was with. I was one of the only queer-identifying people and I was the only trans person. I had left behind my queer community and chose to prioritise my Jewish community for the year, but I definitely missed embracing that aspect of my identity. When I found out we were going to be in another seminar with people in our youth movement from Israel and North America and there were going to be two other transgender guys attending, I was incredibly excited. I loved that being transgender didn't have to define who I was in every aspect and that I could fit in with non-queer people, but that didn't mean it wasn't lonely sometimes. I couldn't wait to meet these other trans men and discuss our transitions. I thought it was amazing that my movement had other trans people in it, and to me that solidified there was a safe place for me within this community.

I met the trans guys and straight away compared myself to them. I wanted to see who looked more "believably" like a man. Then I felt guilty for even thinking about it. After speaking with them briefly, I realised we had little in common. We discussed transition-related topics, then there wasn't much more we could talk about. Conversation didn't flow like I thought it would and I didn't feel very connected to them. I realised that just because we may have had certain aspects of our identity in common, this didn't mean we were destined to be friends. It reminded me of when I was a lesbian and people would say, "Oh, you're a lesbian? I have a lesbian friend you should meet!" Being part of the same marginalised group means there is a certain solidarity and shared experience, but it's not the only factor that contributes to a strong relationship.

* * *

Being a trans person in Israel had some interesting moments. Aside from the very blatant misgenderings I encountered without the social filter I had become accustomed to in Australia, there was also the aspect of religion. I was not heavily involved in the religious world either at home or in Israel. I don't consider myself particularly religious. I am deeply and wholly Jewish, but for me that is more to do with the culture, language, music, food and engagement in community, than the religion.

For a few months, my program had us based in Jerusalem, and suddenly I was confronted with the Jewish religion in a way I had managed to avoid throughout my transition. The moment I realised this was on a trip to the Western Wall, one of the holiest places for the Jewish people. The Wall is divided into two parts: the men's section and the women's. I was already feeling displaced there. I had been to the Wall before and was told I would have some sort of transcendent spiritual and religious feeling, which I didn't, so I was underwhelmed to be there again. I had only ever been to the women's section (which for the record is about half the size of the men's) and I was afraid to enter the men's, considering I wasn't passing as frequently in Israel as I was used to. I decided both for spiritual reasons and gender-related safety that I wouldn't go up to the Wall; I would watch from afar and ask my friends how their experiences were.

Not going up to the Wall was the right decision for me at the time, but I had a lot less choice when it came to needing to pee. I headed straight for the men's toilets and was glared at by the men in long black coats and big fluffy hats. It was terrifying. I thought I might be arrested.

Over the months that we lived in Jerusalem, I became accustomed to being stared at, feeling unsafe in religious spaces and sometimes even being yelled at. As a group, we often went into the homes of religious people. These generous, beautiful people opened their homes to travellers or non-citizens who needed a place to go to for Friday night dinner, which is a time for Jewish people to come together with family, take a break from the week and be close to each other. Growing up with family dinners every Friday night, it can feel like a very lonely time when away from home, and these people took it upon themselves to create an open house for anyone in need. These were people I would rarely encounter in my usual life. I was grateful to be in their homes but I felt like I had to hide away from them as a trans person. I was cautious every time I opened my mouth, in case anything I said would accidentally indicate my trans or queer identity.

In the Jewish religion, men and women are not allowed to touch each other before marriage, unless they are family. It was affirming when religious men shook my hand – it meant they were seeing me as a man. Though in the same moment I felt guilty, as if I was tricking them into committing a sin. I wasn't sure how Jewish law navigated non-normative gender identities, if at all.

I did go to the Western Wall on the men's side one day and ignored the stares that came my way. It wasn't a heartfelt or revolutionary moment; I simply felt out of place.

Nevo at their brother's wedding, nineteen years old (2015)

Chapter 11
Here, Queer and Jewish

I had been away for around eight months when my mum came to Israel to visit me. My mum and I were in contact most days through the glorious modern technologies of WhatsApp, Skype, Viber and Facebook. She was fairly updated on my program, my journey and my feelings, and had been watching my YouTube videos so she could follow the changes I was experiencing on testosterone. I was eager for her arrival and looking forward to spending some time on weekends and holidays getting away from a household of sixteen people.

It was amazing to be reunited, but even though Mum had been watching my videos, she wasn't quite prepared for how hairy I would be. I met up with her at the LGBTQIA+ Pride Parade in Jerusalem and the first thing she commented on when she saw me was my facial hair.

Then I showed her my stomach and leg hair …

I decided while Mum was in town I should do something for my YouTube channel and conduct an interview between us. I had received a few questions specifically in relation to my mum and our relationship, and I thought it'd be fitting to make a video. We sat on the rooftop of the place where we were staying in Tel Aviv and had a very relaxed conversation about my transition and our relationship. Mum was drinking a coffee and I was reading questions from my phone. Neither of us ever anticipated that the video would get over 3000 views. It was only the two of us, having a chat, with lots of banter and a very real insight into our life together.

* * *

I had been feeling more and more comfortable in my body since starting testosterone. My reflection made more sense and I felt like I fit into my skin in a way I had never felt before. One day, my housemates and I were playing around with nail polish and I decided to put some on. It had been years since the last time I had worn it and I wasn't sure how I would feel. My hands had been a point of dysphoria because they were slender and what I viewed as "feminine". I tried to keep the nail polish on for a while. When I went to the supermarket I noticed people were staring at me.

Since more changes were happening heads had stopped turning every time I walked down the street and I didn't feel like I was constantly attracting attention. I had become relaxed in my invisibility, so I thought it would bother me that people were staring again, but it didn't.

Although it had been a nice change not to have people constantly looking at me, I eventually felt strange blending in with everyone else. I never felt "normal" and I wasn't sure I ever would be or would want to be. I was interested in re-exploring my queer identity and felt safe enough in the way I was being read to push the limits a bit further and begin to present more visibly alternative. I had gotten to the point where I was done being invisible. I'd spent too long pretending I was like everyone else. I started wearing nail polish more consistently and worked to stop hating the things that were feminine about myself, but rather, embrace them.

* * *

I have only ever been me. Sometimes, I have been more authentically myself, but I have only ever transitioned from me to a better version of me. I don't identify with the words "female" or "male". They are not my words. The space in which I have felt gendered female and transitioned to gendered male has been in the ways people have treated me.

The changes I experienced on testosterone were significant. With every month throughout my year in Israel, I knew I had made the right decision to be on testosterone. Yet I think the biggest change was less the physical attributes and more how the world treated me as a man, compared to as a woman.

It is undeniable that the world is an easier place to live in for men. The only reason anyone would contest that would be a lack of perspective. If you are a person of colour, transgender, from a lower socioeconomic background, or have different physical or mental capabilities, then of course this affects how difficult life and the world is for you. But on the privilege/oppression dynamic between men and women, it is men who hold the power and women who are the marginalised group. Men are afforded more space, more money and more rights.

Privilege is a very difficult thing to see through privileged eyes. I am privileged in many ways and this has allowed me access to countless rights and opportunities. Acknowledging this addresses the fact that there are power imbalances in our society, which require change. One of the first steps in overturning the white heteropatriarchy to which many of us are victim is admitting it exists, and that we are complicit in the oppressions it produces, even if we don't consciously oppress. Only then can we try to navigate processes to overcome it.

People have argued with me against feminism. They have tried to convince me there are no differences between men and women in our society. While this may be the experience of some, that does not make it the truth. I can give tangible examples of how people's interactions with me have changed since my transition.

When I identified as a woman, I was often called "sweetheart", "darling" and "honey". I never liked those labels. They created a power imbalance where the person calling me that was asserting some kind of dominance over me. I was no one's "sweetheart". I think this feeds the societal expectation that women should be polite, quiet and lovely – a sweetheart. I come from a long line of loud and not particularly polite women, and I'm proud of that. Often men would speak over me, interrupt me and say things similar to if not the exact thing I had just said. I rarely walked home alone at night. Even during the day I felt scared passing strange men on the street. I made sure I was always accompanied, that someone always knew where I was, and I would have fake conversations on the phone while walking past people to seem less vulnerable. I had adjusted to being afraid of men. It was just an expected reality.

I felt a large shift in how I was treated when I was read as a man. I was suddenly referred to as "bro", "mate" and "dude", which made me feel accepted into some sort of covenant. Those words reflect a certain closeness and level of friendship that "sweetheart" and "honey" do not. I suppose I started to feel a brotherhood with men that I had never felt before. I felt taken more seriously by men. If I said anything about feminism, I felt listened to, compared to being trivialised when I was presenting as a woman. People laughed at my jokes more and I was allowed more space to speak. There was a new energy when walking home at night. I felt safer, and I realised that when I was walking behind women, it was possible I had come to be perceived as a threat myself. I had to be aware of what being read as a man would mean for women. I started crossing the road and avoiding situations that could make a woman feel unsafe. These were not privileges I had anticipated or ever wanted, but I had a new responsibility in recognising how a society that favours men would favour me when read as one of them.

People stopped commenting on my weight and the clothing I wore. Comments became more focused on how strong I was rather than how skinny, or how nice my shirt was. There was less pressure on my appearance because suddenly I was valued for the content of my personality, rather than my physical attributes. I could grow my body hair out without being stared at, wear the same outfit every day without anyone saying anything or even noticing. After my transition, my mum even asserted that now I was the man of the house, I would have to do some heavy lifting. I went from one rigid gender box to another, but this one had more space.

* * *

After the final months of my program in Israel and a brief stint in Europe and Thailand, I came home. I hadn't been in Australia for almost a year and was both ecstatic and petrified to be back. I couldn't wait to see my friends and family, but I was scared to come home to a world very different from what I had been immersed in. My mum, brother and sister surprised me at the airport. I was overwhelmed and excited to see them. But seeing familiar people after a year apart was strange. Following an extended period of living with gender as an underlying silent current, it was quickly brought to the forefront again. Everyone commented on my facial hair, deep voice and other changes they noticed. I had to deal again with people using the wrong name and pronouns for me, which I hadn't experienced for a long time. I was asked a lot of questions about my transition. I longed to become invisible again.

I felt quite displaced after I got home. Mum had moved out of our apartment to go travelling and hadn't found a new place by the time I was back, so we were housesitting. I was suddenly living with a parent again and needing to check in about where I was going and what I was doing. Everything was hauntingly quiet. Living in a house with two people is quite different to a house of sixteen, and I felt lonely. I went to my old family home to visit my dad and his new wife. My dog ran up to me and sniffed me, but it was clear she didn't know who I was. I looked different, smelled different, sounded different. It was a bittersweet moment because it meant that I had changed. I was truly becoming the person I felt inside, yet I worried about being unrecognisable. Sometimes I looked in the mirror and I wasn't sure I even recognised myself. I didn't want to lose who I used to be completely.

I had been so preoccupied while overseas that it seemed my body had changed without my mind having time to catch up. I welcomed the changes. Though it was strange to look back on old photos of myself and no longer be sure who I felt more like: the person I was used to being, or this new me. I had to readjust to what I looked like and spend some time getting to know myself as a man, or at least a person with new characteristics and a new identity in society. While everyone was getting to know the person I had become, I was doing the same.

I reunited with close friends that I had been apart from for too long. I spent time coming to terms with the fact that Tia and I would not be rekindling our relationship. It turned out a year away is a year out of touch with reality.

When I came back, it hit me hard that we would not be together. While I mourned a loss I hadn't expected to affect me a year later, Tia had moved on. We eventually reconnected and started a strong friendship. I got a new job, started dating new people and got ready for university. I wrote some music and got back into the swing of things at Habo.

I began reading a lot about the ideas of different relationship structures – polyamory and ethical non-monogamy – and applied these principles to the new relationships I was in. I tried to re-immerse myself in the queer community by making new queer friends and involving myself in queer and intersectional feminist activism. I took the time to settle into life back in Melbourne.

* * *

2015 – The Transgender Tipping Point

Not only were my friends and family interested in talking about my transition after being away, but it seemed the whole world had suddenly become interested in talking about transgender people. When I came out in 2013, there was very little media attention around transgender topics. By 2015 it seemed the mainstream was ready to start talking about issues of gender and sexuality more deeply. This was a huge moment for the transgender community. To see my identity at the centre of discourse was incredible, and also scary. This sudden exposure meant that not only was I hearing important conversations, but also more negative comments than ever. The transphobia flung at celebrities like Caitlyn Jenner and Laverne Cox over social media may not have ever reached them, but it reached me and many other young trans people. It was painful to gain this visibility in transness, because it meant there was also more visibility in transphobia.

A few years prior, while I was still at school, I was included in a few documentaries, and these weren't screened until 2015. The first was called "Love in Full Colour" by Suzi Taylor. It's a beautiful film that follows the stories of multiple young queer students and their experiences in school. It also focuses on Minus18's same-sex and gender diverse formal. The documentary was filmed over two years and I was pleased to see it was to be screened at the Melbourne Queer Film Festival. I was asked to be on a Q&A panel afterwards. I knew it would be confronting to see old footage of myself, but I wasn't the only one who had transitioned since the film, and I anticipated that I would not be alone in this apprehension.

We sat together and cringed as different versions of ourselves popped onto the big screen. I was nervous about seeing the old me. I was blonde, identifying as a lesbian and talking about how I wanted to spend the rest of my life with Tia. I was different now. I had come a long way, but I still had a lot of respect for the journey I was on at that time.

The host of the Q&A was a journalist with a show on Radio National, and a few months later she asked my mum and me to be interviewed. From there, things began to snowball. I received calls every few weeks for a different interview both in general mainstream media and within the Jewish community. I was excited to be received with such acceptance and interest, but it was quite a shift from not having spoken about these topics for some time. The language surrounding many of the interviews was incorrect and, to an extent, hurtful. I understood that society had a way to go in transgender education before everyone gets it right. I have always seen it as my responsibility to be part of that education. I felt like it was important for me to take those opportunities to both provide insight for people who may not understand, but also to be a role model for young transgender kids who may feel they don't have a future – like I used to feel.

* * *

Mum and I were asked to speak at a Jewish Women's group. We tried to prepare for the speech but knew our story would have to be told naturally, improvising and interrupting each other. That first speech we did together was probably one of my most meaningful and deeply personal pieces of activism thus far. We were in a room, surrounded by one of the demographics I had struggled with the most in my life – older Jewish women. Mothers of kids who had bullied me, who didn't make play dates when my parents went away; conservative women with their belief in gender binaries and modesty, sitting down for over an hour and listening to my mum and I talk about our journey through transition. The room was silent. I wasn't sure if people were bored or engaged.

At the end, there was a huge round of applause and had testosterone not put an end to tears, I probably would have cried. The women stayed back, asking us questions and trying to understand better. Many of them approached me, congratulated me and thanked me for teaching them something they knew very little about. An older woman said she would be proud to have me as her grandson, that I was an incredible young man. I was humbled. Although the speech had taken a lot of emotional labour and at some points felt like relived trauma, I felt re-energised from the reaction I received.

Mum and I went on to do more speeches within the community. I was asked to speak at some Jewish high schools, including an event at my old school where I had been severely bullied. I went to a graduate education class at a university as well as a few public and non-Jewish private secondary schools. I had the opportunity to tell my story to many different people. The struggle always came in knowing when to take a break. I was sometimes invigorated and sometimes incredibly drained. Retelling stories you may wish to forget can be very difficult.

Nevo on a Habonim camp, twenty years old (2016)

CHAPTER 12
A Path to Unlearning

I was desperate to get chest surgery. While still in Israel I organised an appointment to see a surgeon. A week after I returned home, I had my first consultation. I was overwhelmingly excited. We consulted briefly, he looked at my chest, took some photos and we made a date for surgery. I had to provide a letter from my psychiatrist but the process was relatively simple. Getting the money to pay for surgery, however, was not. I was lucky enough to be born in a country that recognises chest surgery for trans people is not elective, and Medicare covers a certain amount. I was also fortunate my dad had very good private healthcare under which I was still covered. A surgery that could have cost around $9000 would cost me $6000, with an added rebate of about $1500. For someone who had just arrived back from overseas, was struggling to find work and studying full time, $4500 was a lot of money.

I booked my surgery for July and worked hard to save up the money. I was no longer as dysphoric about my chest. I was able to be topless around people without as much discomfort or self-consciousness. I didn't feel I had to wear my binder around the house as strictly as I once had. I felt a lot better about my body and myself . . . though I still wanted the surgery. I had always wanted a flat chest. I never connected to or appreciated my breasts; they were always a point of insecurity and discomfort. However, I struggled during this stage. I was slowly detaching from the label of "man" and I had to take a step back to consider the reasons for this surgery. I ended up cancelling my July surgery date. It seemed clearer to me the closer it got that I needed to think more about this irreversible decision. Besides, I definitely wasn't going to have saved enough money by then.

A few years prior I had set up a crowdfunding site to help raise the money I would need for testosterone. I didn't like asking for handouts. I worked hard for my money and wanted to pay my own way, but I recognised that it was okay to ask for help. I was dealing with expenses non-trans people would never have to confront. I wasn't forcing anyone to donate and anything that people were capable of giving would make a huge difference to me. So I set up another crowdfunding site for surgery and received overwhelming support. It was this money that made it possible for me to get the surgery. Although I still paid for the vast majority myself, seeing the Jewish community support me in my struggle was inspiring. I couldn't be more grateful to those who donated.

I had a lot of discussions and spent a long time thinking. It was important for me to understand that having a flat chest wouldn't make me "more of a man" or even more masculine. I could identify as a man who had breasts, but I couldn't see a future in which I wouldn't bind my chest. The idea of binding for the rest of my life was suffocating and unhealthy. I didn't want to struggle to breathe any more and I wanted a flat chest. I was working as a swimming teacher and I wanted to be able to lift kids without worrying about my binder ripping open and them freaking out. I wanted to take my shirt off in the change rooms without hiding behind a towel or dashing to the cubicles as I had done as a child.

This was an important surgery. It didn't have to be because I hated my current chest or even because of gender, it was something I felt would improve my life. So I decided to get the surgery.

Leading up to chest surgery I thought I would get super fit. I would eat completely clean, meditate, do yoga and make sure I was the most physically prepared I could possibly be. I didn't do any of that. Life got in the way.

With surgery on the horizon I took off work for a little while and prepared for a few weeks of me-time. I was going to be in hospital for a few days and then I'd be able to come home. I was expecting a huge reliance on my mum and a difficult recovery of about six weeks. At the same time I was also one of the heads of an upcoming Habo camp and had a lot to organise so that I could afford to take some time off after surgery. I've never been particularly good at "time off".

My surgery was taking place in the same hospital I was born in. People kept saying it was momentous, as if I was having a "rebirth". But I didn't feel that way. I hated the idea of marking anything in my transition as a new life – my old life was just as important as this one. On the day of surgery I went to the hospital with my mum and Leila. I was freaking out. I had never been to a hospital outside of my birth and didn't know what to expect. The most comforting advice I was given was that this was the surgeon's job. Although it was a huge deal for me, it was just another day of work for him and all the nurses. All I needed to do was show up and they would do the rest. My mind was eased over this thought. The nurse put a dinosaur strap around my arm before putting in an IV. It was the same strap I've used for every blood test. I've always thought it was cute and seeing something familiar in such an alien space was a small but important comfort. She gave me a gas mask and told me to count back from 10.

10 … 9 … 8 … 7 …

* * *

Mainstream media loves the "born in the wrong body" narrative. I was not born in the wrong body. I was born in *my* body. I am not saying that is every trans person's opinion. It is valid to feel that way. But I do not. I don't believe there is any way my own body could be wrong, except for the ways society has tried to poison my view. It is as if the only way for people to understand transgender individuals is by emphasising there is something wrong with them. By pathologising these identities we shift focus from society's issues onto the issue of the individual.

There was no mistake with my birth. I don't believe that I should have been assigned male at birth and I don't believe that I was born a girl either. By identifying as someone who was assigned female at birth, rather than born a girl, I shifted the conversation from me, onto society.

The only trans people I had ever seen in the media were born a certain gender and became another one. They asserted they were born in the wrong body and that they needed to fix that. There was a time when I believed these things – when I looked in the mirror and didn't recognise who was staring back. I think to a large extent that wasn't necessarily innate, but rather a learned hatred, from a lifetime of indoctrination. It was only days before my chest surgery where I was able to use the words "breasts", a word from which I had detached a long time before.

I wrote a letter to my breasts, to try to encapsulate the deeply complex relationship we'd had:

To my breasts,

Firstly, I want to say I'm sorry. I tried really hard to make it work, and I know you did too. But I'm afraid it was just never meant to be. I think we spent a lot of time and effort trying to get along and feeling upset when it didn't work out, and even though I believe we could have saved a lot of time if we hadn't tried so hard, I'm glad it happened because I think it's gotten us to this point where we can part on good terms.

I really do see you as a friend and I know you never intentionally tried to hurt me. I know it was hard for you to see how much pain I was in as a result of your presence sometimes, but I want you to know it wasn't your fault. You did everything you could. You got smaller, you even grew some hairs so that maybe I would feel less uncomfortable about you. You cooperated with me when I put you into constricting positions that I'm sure you didn't enjoy. And I really do appreciate everything you did.

Honestly, I'll probably miss you. I think I tried to convince myself for a long time that I wouldn't and that it would just be easier to hate you, but I'm not sure I can do that any more.

I don't hate you, I respect you, and we've been through a lot together. I know it was hard for both of us when we were younger and started getting told to cover up. I know we've always been confused as to why we can't go out in public together. I know that you've had your own challenges within yourself, being asymmetrical was hard for you growing up and I know I wasn't always the most supportive about it.

I need you to know that I'm not saying goodbye because I don't love you. I think we've just gotten to this point where we need to move on. And I know this is probably hard for you to hear, but I do believe I'll be happier without you. I also think this will be better for you. You need to be free and I'm just going to keep holding you back and pushing you down. It's time to separate.

So please know that I will miss you. And I'll probably think about you from time to time. And I'm grateful that I had you in my life as long as I did, because you presented me with challenges that made me grow and develop as a person. Good luck for the future, and I hope you can forgive and understand.

Lots of love and respect,

Nevo

* * *

When I woke up I wasn't sure if the surgery was over or

not. I felt completely lucid, and looked around the room waiting for someone to notice I was awake. After a little while a nurse told me it was over; I had done a great job. They brought me back to my room where my mum and Leila were waiting. My chest felt tight as it was wrapped up with bandages and a surgical binder. The surgery was a huge success. I read some letters from my friends, watched some TV shows and went to sleep.

The few days I had in hospital were nice. I wasn't in any pain and didn't take any of the painkillers I was offered except Panadol. The nurses woke me up at different intervals to check various things. I had visitors consistently while I was there. I felt loved, inundated with messages of support. People brought food, flowers and USBs filled with things I could watch.

After a few days I was told I could take a shower. It was time to see my chest for the first time. My hands were shaking as I undid the zip of my surgical binder. I expected to see a wounded battlefield. Big, red gashes across my chest; my battle scars. I took the binder off, unwrapped the bandages and opened my eyes in the mirror. It was swollen but it was beautiful. No battlefield. No casualties. Just me and the chest I had always wanted. It was still fresh but I could finally see it. I had waited my whole life for this moment. I couldn't stop smiling. After my shower the nurse asked if I was okay.

I was great.

* * *

The road to recovery was faster than I expected. I was up and about almost immediately and I felt good. When I finally saw my scars under the tape that had been holding them together I was shocked as to how thin they were. The surgical binder was the hardest part of it all. It was terribly tight and hurt my back, but after so many years of wearing a binder, I could handle a few more weeks. Wearing a T-shirt for the first time without a binder and still having a flat chest was surreal. I kept waiting for my breasts to return, an unwelcome and obnoxious guest. But they didn't. My chest just kept healing and becoming more a part of my body. There are still times when I look in the mirror and cannot believe what I'm seeing. There are other times I take it for granted. My nipple sensation never came back, so sometimes it feels like I have an intruder in my body, like this chest is not mine. But whenever I look at it, it feels right. I know I made the right decision.

I was more comfortable in myself than I had ever been. This gave me new possibilities of exploring my gender, my femininity, my style and also my sexuality. I had spent so long crafting the man I wanted to be that I was finally at a point where I could just discover who I was. My attraction to only women started to change. I met more queer people and began feeling attracted to people of all genders. I experimented with make-up, dresses and different ways of expressing myself. It was nice to feel so comfortable in my body that I could do these things without feeling it invalidated my gender. People were confused, but for the first time, I wasn't.

Nevo with their co-worker, at work as a swimming teacher (2016)

CHAPTER 13
The Future is Femme

The more I thought about my gender and the more I was passing as male, the more I realised I wasn't a man. There was always a hesitation I felt when saying I was a man, as if I knew it wasn't the entire truth. I felt I would only be taken seriously if I was transitioning from one to the other. If I had said I wanted certain masculine attributes but still to be the same person, or that I wanted to find medical interventions to ease my dysphoria, no one would have understood.

As it was, I had to prove my certainty to my family constantly, a certainty I could never truly have had. My family would not have understood any ambiguity. They had brought up valid questions about my gender when I was at the early stages of transition, but those questions needed to come from me, not from people by whom I felt unsupported. I needed them to listen to my feelings, to give me the space to explore my identity more freely. I was finally at a point where I had that space and a comfort both in myself and in how the world was treating me, so I could explore how I actually felt in my gender. I didn't understand or fit in with men and I felt that being read as a cisgender man erased parts of me. I was constricted by yet another set of rules and expectations associated to gender. I went from the rigid box assigned to women to the one assigned to men, and I couldn't fit into either.

I didn't want to reject my masculinity. It was something I had spent such a long time coming to terms with and embracing. But I didn't fit in with men. I didn't get along with them in the way I did with women and even though I was treated better by them, I still didn't always feel safe. Being read as a man, I was usually read as a straight man, which completely erased my queer identity. When I was read as a gay man, I felt like it didn't fully encompass the complexity of my history and identity. It was at this time I discovered the term "non-binary".

Maybe I was neither male nor female, man or woman. Maybe the idea of gender is socially constructed through institutions and social norms we've created. Gender has changed through time, cultures and geographies. Once I recognised this, a liberating thing happened. I started to look at myself as a human being, who is a mix of masculinities and femininities, interests that transcend gendered behaviour, and intricate relationships and emotions that cannot be sorted into simply "male" and "female". So I came out again, for about the fourth time. This time, not as a lesbian, not a transgender man, or queer. This time I came out as me.

* * *

I asked people to do their best not to gender me, but rather treat me as a human being they know and understand. I began reclaiming the femininity I had repressed for so long. I wanted to meet myself again. I moved from nail polish to glitter, eyeliner, lipsticks, mascara and eventually dresses. It became quite difficult getting dressed every morning. I wasn't sure if halfway through the day of wearing a dress, I would suddenly feel masculine again and want to take it off. I had to err on the edge of discomfort most of the time.

I felt anxiety in relation to being read as a cisgender masculine man, which I never expected to feel. But at the same time if I presented too femininely, I ran the risk of feeling the old anxiety I held when I was in my early transition stage. Again I developed some self-hatred and depression. I was upset that I couldn't simply be happy. I had gone through a lot to get to this point, but I realised much of it revolved around how others would perceive me.

While that's completely valid, it sucks. I wish I could have focused more on how I felt, detached from the perceptions and judgements of others.

Reclaiming my femininity was a long process. I met with disapproval from wider society and a lack of understanding from my family. They had finally grasped I was a man; they couldn't begin to process the idea of me existing outside a narrow gender binary. I didn't want to push them. It had been hard enough to earn the acceptance I had. I didn't want to lose it. To my family I remained their son, their brother and their "bro". I have accepted that it is unlikely certain family members will ever refer to me with they/them pronouns. I wanted only to be treated as a human. I didn't want the associated expectations of being a woman or a man. At Friday night dinners my more distant relatives tried to offer me a kippah, and when I rejected the proposition they got angry with me, so I chose the path of least resistance, which was to be a man. It's still a big step from what it used to be, but not quite how I feel comfortable. However, I think we all have to make some compromises sometimes for our families, and most people don't feel entirely comfortable with theirs.

It was hard for my mum to see me in a dress. She had spent much of my childhood trying to make me into the daughter she wanted and it hurt her that I had rejected it strongly. To see me now, trying to embrace my femininity, was painful for her. I didn't understand that at the time, and her expectation I would conform to conventional masculinity confused me. I thought we had moved past these rigid gender roles. But I now understand it took her a long time to process who I was as a man. That it would take a lot longer to come to terms with the fact I could be a feminine man, or someone with an even more complicated relationship with gender.

When I presented as feminine in public, the space around me swelled, as if people were afraid to come too close and catch my trans-ness. I hadn't been visibly trans in years and it brought back a lot of past distress. People wouldn't sit next to me on the train. I got yelled at, "Are you a boy or a girl?" as if those were my only options. I was threatened, honked at, catcalled and made to feel as if I didn't belong. I wasn't trying to make a political statement. This wasn't about ideology.

I still didn't know how to fit in the world. Some days I felt the only thing that could get me out of the house was wearing a dress and feeling pretty. I'm not sure why, that's just the way it was. It was constantly scary. I suffered depression and anxiety in my second year of university. I didn't know what I wanted any more. I knew I loved the results of testosterone, but I wanted to be treated with more complexity than simply as a man. I was more than that.

I ran out of educational energy. I had received so many

questions for so many years and the more I answered them, the less certain I was of the answers. Even when not experiencing explicit transphobia and hatred, the act of living in a society that asserts there is a certain standard to which you must subscribe can be distressing.

* * *

Towards the end of 2013, the year I had come out as trans, a friend of mine asked if I wanted to be involved in a documentary project. I had already done some work with Minus18 and the Safe Schools Coalition and was always excited to get involved in other community-based initiatives. I was interviewed at her house about my process of transition and didn't think that much about the project. I certainly did not anticipate it would become a national resource in schools to help understand LGBTQIA+ issues and provide information to anyone interested. I also didn't expect it would be such a point of controversy.

When the resource came out in 2015, there was a huge backlash. People were angry about the program and claimed that it was indoctrinating children. They argued that kids who were against gay and transgender people no longer had a space to express their feelings at school. There was mass media coverage, protests and counter rallies. The program was pulled from many schools and an investigation commenced to decide whether it adhered to the curriculum and was age appropriate. The report found that it was, but still funding was cut and representatives from Safe Schools were verbally attacked and defamed.

Here is what I think of the Safe Schools program: Safe Schools saved my life. I'm honestly not sure what my future would have been had my high school not been a part of the Safe Schools Coalition and had a club specifically for queer students. To see it being ripped down publicly and ignorantly was devastating. It was also very personal. There was no recognition in the discourse of how harmful these critiques would be for young people desperate for the resource. State-sanctioned homophobia would be the terrifying result.

This was one of the moments where my personal and political selves met at a very tense intersection. It was a scary and triggering time for me. My video was just me, at seventeen, talking about my process and trying to offer some advice that may help gender diverse young people feel more supported. I had to avoid the media for a while and try not to read too much into what was happening. But because I was the subject of one of the lesson plans, all of these attacks felt deeply personal.

The Australian Christian Lobby wrote targeted articles about me. I felt quite hopeless. I was putting myself out there, exposing myself, coming out to the world, and getting hatred and anger in return. Part of me wanted to hide in a cave for the rest of my life. I spent many months experiencing bad mental health while balancing work, university, Habo volunteering, friendships and as much activism as I could handle. Then when I felt I was getting on top of things again, the articles came out. They specifically quoted me and named me, referred to me as "the transgender" and said I was encouraging "sex change surgeries" for kids without parental consent. I had never done such a thing. I didn't know what "sex change surgery" even was. There are many different surgeries available to trans people and they often involve a long process to gain access to them. Even though I was old enough to consent to my chest surgery without parental involvement, my parents were a large part of my surgery because I wanted them to be. They had been with me throughout my process. The articles were pure slander. They threw me straight back into a pit of depression and anxiety. I wondered if there would ever be a safe place for people like me.

* * *

I have a lot of anger. Anger fuels my activism. It gives me power on days when I feel I can't go on. I am angry at many aspects of society, and I have every right to be. As a young girl, while boys around me play-fought and rolled around aggressively and it was shaken off as "boys will be boys", I was taught to repress my anger. When I would get upset or angry about things I was told I was being too emotional.

I had a lot of anger issues as a child. I think it was the direct result of feeling totally lost and misunderstood, but I bullied people and I was constantly aggressive. I spent a long time trying to dull those feelings, ignore them and hide them. It is within the last few years that I have learned to redirect them. I don't think anger is an inherently bad emotion. I think some of the actions that come from it certainly can be, but I think redirection rather than invalidation has worked best for me.

When I have conversations about gender, sexuality, feminism and oppressive forces in our society, I get angry. I get angry because a lot of these things affect me on a deeply personal level on a daily basis. I can't have objective dispassionate conversations about these topics and I don't want to. I get into debates surrounding these ideas and people try to shift the conversation away from the topic and towards my emotions. They say, "You're being too emotional" and "Can't we have a rational conversation?" or "If you weren't being aggressive about this, maybe more people would agree." I understand where those sentiments come from, and maybe for the most productive discussion certain standards should be upheld, but that's easy to say when those issues are not yours. If you don't experience those oppressions, you don't get to have an opinion on how they affect the people that do.

The oppressive gender forces in society constantly distress me; they have triggered, traumatised and destroyed me in many ways. I don't want to talk about them without emotion. It is absurd to expect people of oppressed minorities to calm themselves and educate you delicately on a topic you don't understand because you haven't put in the effort. It takes enough energy for us to exist. It is what we in the Jewish world would call a chutzpah – a stronger word for audacity that means having the "guts" to say something you probably shouldn't.

* * *

I still struggle every day getting onto public transport and seeing the uniforms that have been pre-approved for men and women. When everyone looks the same, your differences become acutely obvious. Depending on the day, it can feel empowering, but other times it feels raw and exposing. People's stares might be interpreted in my mind as envy, or attraction, but on the worst days, I see hatred, violence and disgust.

I have also had to work hard to find healthy and authentic ways to express my masculinity. Most representations surround patriarchy, dominance and toxic understandings of what it means to be masculine. But it's important for me to recognise who I am, break down the binary understandings of both masculinity and femininity and find a comfortable spot that fits for me.

I have spent many years trying to unlearn what has been ingrained in me. That women and men need to look a certain way; that my future holds marriage and kids; I must find a job I both like and that pays lots of money, and stick with it for my whole life; I need to have a degree; how much money I make is a measure of how successful I am; and other standards that I cannot reach, or don't want to. It's scary to realise that the adults around you aren't always right, or that the life they envision for you does not necessarily apply. It's not easy to unlearn what we have been taught from birth.

For every concept learned that I manage to break down, I discover another I didn't realise was there, making the path of unlearning a never-ending one. I am grateful to exist in an environment where I do have other options than what I've been taught. I have communities that encourage diversity, counterculture and rebellion. Inspirational activists surround me and fuel a belief that things can change, and that they can be better. If you don't think they should and that the way society functions currently is perfectly successful, then it's likely you've never had to think about your privilege. Privilege is often invisible to those who have it. Try looking at the world from another perspective, listen to other people, then reconsider.

* * *

If it wasn't for my youth movement, I think it could have been easy for me to reject my Judaism, move north-side and assimilate into the queer community. I'm grateful that didn't happen. My Judaism is important to me; it's integral to everything I am and it's my community. Despite differences in ideologies and understandings, I trust the Jewish community. I know that should I ever need it, the Jewish community will be there for me.

My life has always revolved around community, and still does. Being raised with many wonderful people in my life has made me feel an important sense of belonging. Engaging in transgender and feminist activism within the Jewish community is vital for me. I have had many young queer Jewish people message me and ask for my help. I have loved being in Habo as a leader. Educating kids on essential and critical issues has made me a better person. I run programs on gender and sexuality, polyamory, privilege, feminism and other issues and there is plenty of space for me to do that.

The queer community is also integral to my existence. I could not comfortably assimilate into the Jewish community without embracing my queer identity. My queerness bleeds into my political position on many issues. In recent years, other trans and gender diverse people have been a lifeline for me in times of dysphoria and depression. Seeing people transcend gender binaries and fight to take them down fills me with inspiration and hope. I am surrounded by incredible activists changing the world. It helps me to keep going.

The queer community is not without its issues. I have spent a long time, and imagine I shall spend a long time in the future, trying to navigate my place in this community and within its politics. I have seen and experienced things that have made me feel unsettled. We need to find ways of engaging in political discussions that don't isolate people if they aren't knowledgeable enough, or happen to make mistakes. Similar to the Jewish community, I feel a responsibility for the problems that exist here. I am committed to changing it for the better, and also taking a step back on issues that don't directly affect me in the hope of supporting those who are affected.

It's amazing to be a part of two incredible communities. I am abundant in love and support. But sometimes, being part of both communities at once can feel tense. It doesn't always feel like I truly belong anywhere. My queer family will never understand what it means to be Jewish, and how I connect to my Israeli identity. At the same time, the Jewish community will never fully comprehend my life as a trans, queer, polyamorous person.

I am always trying to find ways to bring the communities together in my life, but often I am balancing the two on opposite ends of my identity and city – quite literally! I drive from the south-east suburbs to the northern suburbs multiple times a week. I still live with my mum. I am grounded in a community of Jewish people at my workplace, in my neighbourhood and at my movement. I feel like I am always explaining my identity in both worlds. But it's a process and I wouldn't change it. I have also made queer Jewish friends that feel similarly, and we are trying to navigate these two identities together. I hope I'll maintain balance between the two without having to compromise either, because they are both integral to who I am.

* * *

A lot has happened in my short life. It has changed in unimaginable ways and I often have to stop and look at it through the eyes of my younger self in order to truly appreciate it. I have experienced adversity and oppression, but I have also had immense privilege and met incredible people.

I can't be sure what my future will look like – no one can. All I know is I'm doing my best. I have learned so much from the communities I am a part of. A new world of potentials and opportunities and learning has opened up to me.

The world is scary for people like me. I hope you will think about what you can do to try to make that world less scary. People have been inspired by my story and have looked at me as a role model. That's lovely. It means a lot to me. But I don't want to hear how my story has touched you. I would rather hear what you're going to do to make this world safer so that each trans person doesn't need to be a role model. So we can live our lives without being constantly politicised. So we can choose to be activists, not be forced into it.

Nevo on a Habonim camp, twenty years old (2016)

Afterword

I look in the mirror now and I'm not sure if I see a man, a woman, a child, an adult. I guess I just see me. I've always seen me. Sometimes I look more like me, sometimes less. Some days I prefer not to look in the mirror at all. It's difficult to end a story that is still continuing.

I think of my past as fractured, each stage of my life as a different identity. It makes me sad that I will never again meet the people I used to be. I have a lot I'd like to say to them. I wonder how they'd react to me. I find solace in imagining a party where we all attend, and I'd like to share that with you.

* * *

It is almost impossible to decide what to wear. I have no

idea how I want to represent myself. I know everyone will be confused to see me as it is. I don't want to wear a dress; I feel awkward about it. I'm not even sure I can handle make-up. I know part of that decision is because I want to show them how "successful" my transition has been. What a believable man I am capable of disguising myself as. This is not going to be a safe space, even though it will be filled with people I know very intimately.

I settle on a pair of black jeans, an eccentric shirt, my leather jacket and some jewellery. I want to look challenging, to be true to both my masculinity and femininity. I don't want to just make people comfortable, but I'm not in a state to go all out. I put a bit of glitter on. I know it will make me feel better. My lighter necklace dangles against my shirt. I always keep my flame close to me.

I drive up to the venue and don't have trouble parking – after all, I am the only one with a licence. I enter the building and straight away I see six-year-old Liat. His hair is short, but only as short as Mum will let it be. He is wearing a dress he has obviously been forced into for the occasion. He looks up at me and smiles, and starts chattering about something I can't quite understand. I nod along and laugh. He shows me his new skull ring and I tell him it's cool. I say that it's okay if he wants to take the dress off – Mum's not here, it's just us. His face lights up and he quickly sheds the dress to reveal bike shorts and a T-shirt with a dragon on it. He tells me he's a boy, and I believe him. He grabs my hand, touches my beard and gives me a hug. I hold him close and tell him it's going to be okay, he knows who he is, and no one can tell him otherwise. He squeezes me right back, then runs off in a way he couldn't have if he was still wearing the dress.

As I walk further into the room, I notice heads turn. I wonder how many people I have surprised, how many I have impressed and how many I have disappointed. I happen upon nine-year-old Liat. She stands out among the others around her age. She's straightened her hair underneath a train-conductor style hat, and is wearing lip-gloss, a denim mini skirt and a shirt that hangs off her shoulder. I see her staring at other versions of us and wonder who she relates to the most. I wonder if she lusts after the freedom of more masculine Liats, or if she is comfortable in the way she has dressed.

Thirteen-year-old Liat comes up to me and says, "You look different". I nod and am silent because I'm not sure I can say anything without crying. I don't know if I've disappointed her. She has tried so hard to be a woman and she is doing a great job. I worry I have failed her. I miss her but I can see how sad she is behind the mascara she has tried to put on. She pulls at her shirt, attempting to cover the size of her stomach as much as she can. She has been looking around to see if she is skinnier than the others. I tell her she is beautiful, always and forever. She is intelligent and powerful and if she wants to she will change the world. Although she knows I'm right, she has a hard time believing me. She hasn't yet felt loved and desired in the ways she will.

I go over to a mirror with her and ask her to point out her favourite features. She says she likes her hair, it makes her feel unique; she likes her hands because her fingers are slim; her face because it looks like her. I agree with everything she says and realise those things have not changed. I hear her voice drop as she begins to talk about her body and I stop her. "You are a force to be reckoned with. More of you means more space taken up. Your fat is part of your strength, your identity and your image. Own it and be proud." She starts crying. I'm not sure anyone has told her this yet. As I say the words I remind myself that they are still applicable. I know she will have a tumultuous time with her body and weight, but I hope these words will make it easier.

I am overwhelmed. Nothing could have quite prepared me for the emotions I would experience in this space. I feel my heart racing and realise I am probably having an anxiety attack. I'm not sure anything I can say to these people will make a difference. I'm also not certain I am the one with the most wisdom.

I sit down beside other Nevos and Liats. We fiddle with our phones. We message no one, check the time and maybe play a game. Some read over old messages, others plan new ones. We sit in silence. Elsewhere, I would feel awkward in such a silence, as if someone needed to speak soon or it will feel uncomfortable. But we all know why we're here. We need a little time out, and there is a deep understanding among us.

I can see seventeen-year-old Nevo in the corner of the room, shyly eyeing me. I know he wants to come over but can't. I consider going to him then realise I can't either. I pretend not to notice him.

I find sixteen-year-old Liat. She is the most sure of herself and I sit with her a while. She's wearing jeans and a button-up. Her hair is short and curly; she has only recently stopped straightening it. She tells me about Tia, and about her dreams for the future. She wants to be a mum, is thinking of being a psychologist and spends a lot of time writing music. I thought I would have words of wisdom for her but realise that it is the other way around. She is surer of herself than I think I'll ever be. I listen as she speaks excitedly. She talks of love in the kind of unguarded way I can only imagine. I have been stung too many times to speak that way now. She tells me she likes my beard. I knew she would.

I light a cigarette and heads turn. I don't have the energy to explain why dying is less scary to me now. It's not that I want to. It's just that I'm no longer as afraid.

I muster up the courage to speak to seventeen-year-old Nevo. He is anxious, awkward, not sure of himself at all. We notice eighteen-year-old Nevo dancing wildly in the centre of the dance floor. We don't speak for a while and I know he has a million questions for me. I tell him he can ask whatever he wants. He asks me about testosterone, when I started, how it felt, what changes I experienced first. He looks at my chest, asks if he can touch it and wants to see my scars. He follows with many questions about surgery. When did it happen? How was it? Was I frightened? What is it like to not have to bind any more? He touches my chest hair, and my stomach hair. He can't believe his eyes. He tells me it's as if he is looking into a mirror of self-fulfilling prophecy. He is the one I had wanted to meet the most. I needed to see how proud he is. He looks carefully at every detail of my skin and body. The appreciation he shows is one that I try to remember to show myself later. I try to answer all of his questions without showing just how much this interaction means to me. I love him so much, and am so grateful for the choices he made.

Eventually, he looks up at me (only slightly, as testosterone has not made me much taller) and asks, "Well, are you happy?"

I take a deep breath, smile and reply, "I'm certainly trying."

He smiles back and we hug.

I go around a corner and see a long hallway. Although I can't see what is behind all of the doors, I know they are insights into my future. I have no idea what versions of me exist behind those doors. What I am wearing, how I am feeling or how I present my gender. I choose not to look into them, as the security in knowing I have a future is enough comfort to me right now. I back away from the hallway. It's not time to go down there yet.

I go over to two-year-old Liat. She is as cute as the photos. I look at her and wonder: If I could go back and do things differently, would I? She looks up at me and smiles.

I wouldn't change a thing.

Nevo after finishing the second draft of this book (2016)

ACKNOWLEDGEMENTS

To my family – both biological and chosen. Thank you for existing, for trying to learn and expand your understandings and for loving me unconditionally. I owe everything I am to all of you. When waking up in the morning is difficult, I think of your faces, your affection and your genuine care, and things become less hard. I am so lucky to have you.

To my Jewish community, we have had our difficulties but I could not be more grateful to be part of such a loving environment. Thank you for showing me that my queerness and Judaism can coexist in beautiful harmony, and that I am not any less Jewish for expressing myself authentically.

To my queer community, the strength I see from you every day fills me with humility and pride. We are warriors and most of our lives are spent on the battlefields, but we hold each other's hands and create strength in numbers. Discovering my queerness has been the hardest and best thing to happen to me. Do not forget how strong you are, that there are people out there like you, who understand and love you.

And finally, to P!nk, you made me my own hero at a very young age when I had nowhere else to turn. You taught me I was powerful and could be anything I wanted. I loved you, I will always love you, and I thank you for the strength in me your music guided me towards.

GLOSSARY

This glossary is not perfect. It is a reference for how these words function in this book. These definitions are by no means exhaustive, objective, wholly representative, or static.

It is important to note that these terms are derived from a Western colonial framework and may not be applicable or relevant to everyone. The use of them may, indeed, be experienced as violence towards people of colour.

Individuals may have different understandings and relationships with these words. It's important not to make assumptions, and to use the terms that people feel comfortable with.

A

agender: people who are gender-neutral or genderless. Agender falls under the umbrella of non-binary and/or transgender.

asexual: people with thoughts and feelings about the frequency and intensity of sexual attraction/interactions that may vary from the usual assumptions. Some asexual people feel no sexual attraction, while others may find someone aesthetically attractive without feeling any sexual attraction.

B

bar mitzvah: a Jewish coming-of-age ceremony for boys turning thirteen.

bat mitzvah: a Jewish coming-of-age ceremony for girls turning twelve.

bisexual: people who are attracted to two or more genders.

C

cisgender: people whose gender identity is the same as the sex they were assigned at birth.

coming out: publicly expressing a state of being outside of "the norm", for example openly identifying as LGBTQIA+ or polyamorous.

D

dysphoria: this term has been used in this book interchangeably with "gender dysphoria", which is the experience of distress brought about by conflicting emotions about one's gender and body.

fatphobia: the idea that fatness is inherently bad.

feminism: the belief that everyone deserves equal rights and opportunities.

G

gender: the attitudes, feelings and behaviours society associates with biological sex.

gender diverse: people whose gender identity differs from their biological sex. This includes transgender people, non-binary people and other gender variants.

gender identity: the gender you identify with, regardless of your biological sex.

H

heteronormative: pervasive cultural and social structures that promote heterosexuality as the default, "normal", or preferred sexual orientation.

heteropatriarchy: the social and political systems in society that prioritise the dominance of heterosexual men over other genders and sexualities.

heterosexual: people who are attracted only to the opposite gender, for example a man who is attracted to women. Also called "straight".

homosexual: people who are attracted only to the same gender. "Gay" often refers to men, but can include women. Homosexual women are also called lesbians.

I

intersectional: overlapping or intersecting identities and systems of oppression and discrimination.

intersex: an umbrella term for people who are born with a body form that varies from the medical model of what is considered "male" and "female".

L

LGBTQIA+: lesbian, gay, bisexual, transgender, queer, intersex, asexual/agender, plus any other gender identities that may exist in the community.

M

mansplainer: someone who gives an unsolicited explanation in a condescending tone. Most frequently done by men to women, although the term has broadened enough that it is often used regardless of gender.

misgender: intentional or unintentional actions that reveal an incorrect understanding of someone's gender, for example calling someone by a pronoun or name that does not reflect their gender identity.

misogyny: hatred of, or prejudice against, girls and women.

monogamy: a relationship where the person has only one partner exclusively.

N

non-binary: an umbrella term for people whose gender identity does not fit within the binary of male and female.

P

packing: wearing padding or a phallic object in your underwear or pants to give the appearance of having a penis.

passing: being read or seen as someone from a dominant group in society. For example, a transgender man being read as a cisgender man, or a person of colour being read as white.

polyamorous: an umbrella term for relationship formats that are not restricted to monogamy.

Q

queer: an umbrella term that LGBTQIA+ people sometimes use to refer to themselves or their community. Historically an offensive word, it is now being reclaimed by some parts of the community.

S

sex: medically based labels for biological and physical attributes that determine whether you are assigned male, female or intersex at birth.

sexual orientation: romantic or sexual attraction towards people of a particular gender.

T

transgender: people whose gender identity can differ to the sex they were assigned at birth.

transition: the social or medical process of change to one's gender or body. This may or may not include changing your name, dressing and behaving differently, taking hormones or having surgery.

transphobia: fear of or prejudice against transgender people.

Resources

beyondblue • A not-for-profit organisation that works to increase awareness of anxiety and depression in Australia and to reduce the associated stigma. There is specific information and resources for LGBTQIA+ people and Aboriginal and Torres Strait Islander peoples, as well as phone and online support hotlines. **www.beyondblue.org.au**

Gender Dysphoria Clinics • Mental health services that help people experiencing gender dysphoria. These clinics can give mental health assessments and help with referrals for endocrinologists and psychologists. **Google "Gender Dysphoria Clinic" and your state.**

It Gets Better • This project's mission is to communicate to LGBTQIA+ youth around the world that "it gets better" and to inspire the changes needed to improve their lives. **www.itgetsbetter.org**

Kids Helpline • A free, anonymous and confidential phone and online counselling service for young people aged between five and twenty-five. Kids Helpline is available to talk about big or small concerns. **www.kidshelp.com.au** or **1800 55 1800**

Lifeline • A national charity providing 24-hour crisis support and suicide prevention services to people of all ages. An online chat and free directory of local health and community services are also available. **www.lifeline.org.au** or **13 11 14**

Minus18 • Australia's largest youth-led organisation for LGBTQIA+ youth. Minus18 provides mental health and peer mentoring support, online resources and networking opportunities. **minus18.org.au**

National LGBTI Health Alliance • The national peak health organisation in Australia for organisations and individuals that run health-related programs and services focused on LGBTQIA+ people. **www.lgbthealth.org.au**

NonBinary.Org • An education and advocacy network that offers information for and about people who don't fit the gender binary. This website includes an extensive database of definitions of LGBTQIA+ terminology. **nonbinary.org**

QLife • Australia's first nationally-oriented counselling and referral services for LGBTQIA+ people. QLife have phone and web-based services for all ages. **qlife.org.au** or **1800 184 527**

Reach Out • A free online youth mental health service run by an Australian non-profit and developed in partnership with health professionals. The website has information, fact sheets, tools, stories, videos and a forum. **au.reachout.com**

Safe Schools Coalition Australia • A national network of organisations that work with schools to create safe and inclusive environments for LGBTQIA+ students, staff and families. They offer free resources, support, guidance and consultation. School membership is voluntary but highly encouraged. **www.safeschoolscoalition.org.au**

TransWhat? • A clear, concise website that can be used to introduce allies to the concept of being transgender. **www.transwhat.org**

Suggested reading

THIS IS A LIST OF INCREDIBLE WRITERS THAT I THINK MIGHT INSPIRE YOU.

Sara Ahmed • A British–Australian scholar whose area of study is the intersection of feminist theory and queer theory. Sara is the former director of the Centre for Feminist Research and Professor of Race and Cultural Studies at Goldsmiths University of London. Her most recent book is *Living a Feminist Life*. **feministkilljoys.com**

Roj Amedi • An editor, writer and strategist based in Australia. She writes and speaks on a range of issues including public policy, international relations, the arts, culture, literature, race, gender and politics. She is particularly passionate about refugee justice, human rights, feminism and LGBTQIA+ rights. Roj's writing has been published in *Vice*, *The Saturday Paper* and *Right Now* among others.

Simone De Beauvoir • A twentieth-century French writer, existential philosopher, political activist and feminist. Her novels, essays and biographies detailed women's oppression and were a foundation of contemporary feminism.

Kate Bornstein • A celebrated transgender trailblazer, Kate is an American author, playwright and performance artist. Kate has written many books about gender, sex and being queer. **katebornstein.com**

Jax Jacki Brown • An Australian disability and LGBTQIA+ consultant, writer, spoken-word performer and public speaker. She has been published on The Wheeler Centre blog, *Junkee*, *Daily Life*, *The Feminist Observer* and in several anthologies. **fukability.blogspot.com.au**

Judith Butler • An American philosopher and gender theorist whose work has influenced ethics, queer theory, feminist theory and literary theory. She has published numerous books, most notably *Gender Trouble: Feminism and the Subversion of Identity*, which developed her theory of gender performativity.

Maddee Clark • A trans Yugambeh freelance writer living in the Kulin Nation. Her writing has appeared in *Artlink* and *Overland*, and she has presented at several festivals and symposiums. Maddee is currently researching Indigenous speculative fiction and futurism.

Kimberle Crenshaw • An award-winning American civil rights advocate and professor at the UCLA School of Law and Columbia Law School, known for the introduction and development of intersectional theory. She has written many books and articles about race and gender issues.

DARKMATTER • A trans South Asian performance art duo comprised of Alok Vaid-Menon and Janani Balasubramanian, based in New York City. They regularly perform to sold-out venues and at universities and festivals. **www.darkmatterpoetry.com**

Angela Davis • An African–American political activist, educator, scholar and writer, known internationally for her work combating oppression in the US and abroad. Angela's articles and essays have appeared in numerous journals and anthologies, and she is the author of many novels.

Alison Evans • An Australian writer and co-editor of the zine *Concrete Queers*. Their work has been published in various Australian and international publications. They have recently published *Ida*, a young adult (YA) science fiction novel with many gender diverse characters. **alisonwritesthings.com**

Clementine Ford • An Australian feminist writer, social commentator and speaker. Clementine is a columnist at *Daily Life* and a regular contributor to *The Age* and *The Sydney Morning Herald*, exploring issues of gender inequality and pop culture. Her latest book is *Fight Like a Girl*. **clementineford.tumblr.com**

Fury • An Australian writer, agitator, poet and illustrator. Their words can be found on *Overland*, *Guardian*, *Kill Your Darlings* and *Vice*. You can find more of their work at **furywrites.com**

Roxane Gay • An American feminist writer, professor and commentator. Roxane's writing appears in *McSweeney's*, *Oxford American*, *Virginia Quarterly Review* and many other international publications. She is the author of several books, including the *New York Times* bestseller *Bad Feminist*. **www.roxanegay.com**

Nayuka Gorrie • A Kurnai/Gunai, Gunditjmara, Wiradjuri and Yorta Yorta woman writer who works with young Aboriginal and/or Torres Strait Islander people at the National Indigenous Youth Leadership Academy. Nayuka's writing can be found on *Vice*, *Junkee* and The Wheeler Centre blog.

Erin Gough • An Australian author of YA novels and short stories, Erin's writing has been published in *Best Australian Stories*, *The Age* and *Overland*. Her debut novel, *The Flywheel*, is a heart-warming queer romance and has been short-listed for various awards. **www.eringough.com**

Sally Haslanger • The Ford Professor of Philosophy in the Department of Linguistics and Philosophy at MIT in America. She has published several books and numerous articles about feminist theory, political philosophy and metaphysics. **sallyhaslanger.weebly.com**

bell hooks (Gloria Jean Watkins) • An acclaimed American intellectual, feminist theorist, cultural critic, artist and writer. She has published personal memoirs, children's books, poetry collections and cultural criticism. Her work covers gender, race, class and spirituality. **www.bellhooksinstitute.com**

Will Kostakis • An award-winning Australian author and journalist, Will has been published in *The Sydney Morning Herald* and *The Star Observer*. He writes short stories and YA novels with queer characters, and his latest book is *The Sidekicks*. **willkostakis.com**

Benjamin Law • An Australian journalist, columnist and screenwriter, Benjamin has written for *frankie*, *The Monthly*, *The Courier-Mail*, *The Big Issue* and *Crikey*. He is best known for his books *The Family Law*, a memoir that was recently turned into a hit TV series, *Gaysia: Adventures in the Queer East*, an exploration of queer life in Asia, and *Shit Mothers Say*, co-written with his sister Michelle and illustrator Oslo Davis. **benjamin-law.com**

David Levithan • An award-winning American YA fiction author and editor of numerous novels featuring queer characters. His notable books include *Boy Meets Boy*, *Will Grayson, Will Grayson* (co-written with John Green) and *Every Day*. **davidlevithan.com**

Celeste Liddle • An Arrernte feminist writer, social commentator and public speaker living in Victoria, Australia. Celeste has spoken at various festivals and been published on *Daily Life*, *The Guardian* and *Crikey*. **blackfeministranter.blogspot.com.au**

Janet Mock • A multiracial American writer, author and transgender rights activist. She is a former staff editor for *People* magazine and currently a contributing editor for *Marie Claire*. Her first memoir, *Redefining Realness*, was a *New York Times* bestseller. Her next memoir is called *Surpassing Certainty*. **janetmock.com**

Giselle Au-Nhien Nguyen • A Vietnamese–Australian writer, copywriter, digital content producer and public speaker. Giselle writes a regular column for *Daily Life* covering feminism, pop culture, sex, race and relationships. Her writing has been featured in *frankie*, *Rookie* and *The Lifted Brow*, and she has spoken at many festivals. **gisellenguyen.com**

Karen Pickering • An Australian writer, feminist and activist. Karen has been published on *The Guardian* and she is the co-founder of Girls on Film Festival. She has recently published an anthology of women writers reflecting on sex, called *Doing It*.

Beverly Guy Sheftall • An American feminist scholar, writer, editor and the Professor of Women's Studies and English at Spelman College, in Atlanta, Georgia. Her most recent book is *Gender Talk: The Struggle for Equality in African American Communities*.

Mariko Tamaki • A Canadian artist and writer for film, radio, television, stage, Marvel and DC Comics. Mariko's work touches on race, gender and sexuality, and includes YA novels and the award-winning graphic novels *Skim* and *This One Summer* with her cousin Jillian Tamaki. **marikotamaki.blogspot.ca**

Marlee Jane Ward • An Australian writer of short stories and novellas, Marlee's words have been published on The Wheeler Centre blog, *Kill Your Darlings* and *Vice*. Her debut novella *Welcome To Orphancorp* has numerous queer characters and has won several awards. **marleejaneward.com**

Alison Whittaker • A Gomeroi poet, essayist and scholar who currently lives in Sydney on Wangal land. Her work has been published in *Meanjin*, *Vertigo* and *Colouring the Rainbow: Blak Queer and Trans Perspectives*. Her latest book is *Lemons in the Chicken Wire*, a collection of poems.